Praise for Salt Rising Bread

"My friend Marion Cunningham first introduced me to salt rising bread – she had been experimenting with baking it in her kitchen, perhaps for one of her cookbooks. She made me some toast at her house, and it was just unlike anything I'd had before. The taste was something really different and unique. It was absolutely perfect toast – it didn't need anything on it, not even butter. And it made great sandwiches, too!"

~ **Alice Waters,** chef, restaurateur, author of *The Art of Simple Food (I and II)*,
40 Years of Chez Panisse, and others

I must admit that I have fallen under the spell of salt rising bread. It is the quirkiest of breads but, like an expensive white truffle, the earthy aroma and flavor are intoxicating. The more I eat the more I want.

~ **Peter Reinhart,** baker, author of *Bread Revolution*, *The Baker's Apprentice*, and others

"Jenny Bardwell and Susan Brown are carrying on the Appalachian art of creating salt rising bread – allowing all of us to indulge in the fruits of their labor! Their combined talent produces the delicious dense bread with a distinctive flavor unique to salt rising bread that is unlike any other. I'll take mine toasted with a dab of butter, please."

~ **Candace Nelson,** author of the food blog "Candace Lately"

"Salt Rising Bread combines oral history and contemporary cookbook to rescue salt rising bread from undeserved obscurity. For those lucky enough to know it from childhood, Susan and Jenny's book will bring back warm memories. For those of us – like me! – who didn't know salt rising bread as children, Salt Rising Bread introduces the gospel of this delicious treat."

~ **Geoffrey Cameron Fuller,** West Virginian and *New York Times* bestselling author

"Here are a couple of ladies bringing the world of wild microbes together with memories of our grandmothers' grandmothers surviving and thriving. They're dusting off battered bread recipes and sewing them together with science, and it's somehow all so life-affirming! Even if you don't remember salt rising bread, you'll want to. The audacious curiosity cultivated here is, in a word: delicious."

~ **Glynis Board,** Reporter, West Virginia Public Broadcasting

"Smells evoke memories, and one of my fondest childhood recollections is of the pungent aroma of salt rising bread being made. My Aunt Avah of Jane Lew, WV, who believed this magical bread had a special consciousness, told us kids that it would only rise if there was absolute peace and harmony in the home. So we had to be quiet all day and not fight if we were to enjoy it. Only later did I become suspicious about her having an ulterior motive for telling us this! Lots of things have changed since then, but not my fondness for toasted salt rising bread. Kudos to Susan and Jenny for reviving this wonderful tradition and helping me relive my childhood."

~ **Greg Juckett,** MD, MPH, Professor of Family Medicine, West Virginia University

"I think it will be interesting to a lot of people to read about salt rising bread because there are an awful lot of people who never have heard of it, how it came about or where it came from. I started working in a bakery when I was twelve and eventually owned one for many years. We made over twenty different kinds of bread, including salt rising, one of the most unique breads of all."

~ **William E. Crum III,** retired baker, Kansas

SALT RISING
BREAD

SALT RISING BREAD

Recipes and Heartfelt Stories of a Nearly Lost Appalachian Tradition

Genevieve Bardwell | Susan Ray Brown

st. lynn's press

PITTSBURGH

Salt Rising Bread
Recipes and Heartfelt Stories of a Nearly Lost Appalachian Tradition

ISBN-13: 978-1-943366-03-3

Library of Congress Control Number: 2016936358
CIP information available upon request

First Edition, 2016

St. Lynn's Press . POB 18680 . Pittsburgh, PA 15236
412.381.9933 . www.stlynnspress.com

Book Design – Holly Rosborough
Editor – Catherine Dees
Editorial Intern – Christina Gregory

Photo Credits:
JBN Photo – cover photo, pages viii, x, xii, xiv, xviii, xxi, xxii, 3, 4, 6, 10, 15, 16, 29, 30, 31, 32, 38, 45, 46, 51, 53, 66, 69, 71, 72, 73, 74, 75, 78, 79, 82, 88, 94, 95, 97, 98, 101, 102, 108, 123, 124, 134 and 135; Genevieve Bardwell – pages 12, 25, 60, 61, 68, 83, 85, 114, 115 and 120 (bottom); Susan Ray Brown – pages xvi, 17, 21, 22, 23, 35, 45, 46, 50, 55, 56, 58, 64, 65, 80, 93, 110, 111, 112, 113, 130; Chloe Wertz – page 119; Christina Gregory – page 120 (top); photo on page 33 provided by Bullock Museum, Texas; photo on page 34 by Dr. Tom L. Lee (https://commons.wikimedia.org/wiki/File:Alulu_Beer_Receipt.jpg); photos on pages 2 and 91 provided by Van de Kamp's Bakery; photo on page 87 provided by Jack Ward; photos on page 89 and 90 provided by Bill Crum.

MIX
Paper from responsible sources
FSC® C016245
www.fsc.org

Printed in Canada
on certified FSC recycled paper using soy-based inks

This title and all of St. Lynn's Press books may be purchased for educational, business or sales promotional use. For information please write:
Special Markets Department . St. Lynn's Press . POB 18680 . Pittsburgh, PA 15236

10 9 8 7 6 5 4 3 2 1

SUSAN

To my grandmother, Katheryn Rippetoe Erwin,
whose salt rising bread has nurtured
my body and soul for more than 50 years.

JENNY

To Pearl Haines, whom I learned from
and who made salt raisin' for over 90 years.

Table of Contents

℃

To Our Readers

Behind every well-loved food there are stories, often heartwarming ones, about where the food came from and the people whose lives it has touched. Most of our food traditions have come to these shores from other places and other continents. Some have adapted and changed over the years and a few have stayed true to their distant origins. But the food we are writing about in this book didn't arrive with the great immigrant waves. It was born in the hills of Appalachia more than 200 years ago and spread from there along the pioneer wagon trails. *Salt Rising Bread* is the story of this uniquely American bread and the people who have continued baking it in the years since, passing their recipes down lovingly from generation to generation.

We, Jenny and Susan, have baked and loved salt rising bread for a very long time. Without exaggeration, we can say that in the universe of breads, it stands alone. There is nothing else remotely like it in terms of flavor, personality and technique. There is mystery about it in the wild microbes that cause it to rise. It has attitude and holds tantalizing secrets that have never been fully revealed. Sadly, very few people are alive today who know how to make this delicious yeastless bread the authentic way. That is the reason that we took it upon ourselves to be the chroniclers and preservers of this nearly lost tradition.

About Us

Susan, whose family has deep roots in the region, is the founder of the online resource The Salt Rising Bread Project (www.saltrisingbread.net). Jenny is the proprietor of Rising Creek Bakery, which specializes in traditional salt rising bread. The bakery is located in Mt. Morris, Pennsylvania, in the heart of Appalachia. More than twenty years ago, we set out to find and interview the people who still baked salt rising bread, and beyond that, to discover the secrets and the science behind its unique fermentation and memorable aroma, texture and taste. Our search took us from the Appalachian parlors and kitchens of bread-making elders to the laboratory of a renowned microbiologist, to bread museums and the pages of rare cookbooks and pioneer diaries. What we found was a treasure of American culinary lore.

If you grew up loving your grandmother's salt rising bread and you miss it (and her), this book is for you. If you haven't yet had the pleasure of eating salt rising bread and wonder why anyone would write an entire book about it, this book is for you too.

We wish you happy reading, along with your own discovery or re-discovery of this wonderful, tradition-rich bread.

Jenny and Susan

A Salt Rising Bread Memory, Sent to Susan's Salt Rising Bread Project

"I grew up in Spelter, WV, just north of Clarksburg on Rt. 19. My grandmother baked this bread EVERY Saturday morning of her life. I don't think she ever bought bread. She would make several loaves and a couple of cookie sheets full of wonderful large buns. We lived next door and she would call me over just before she took the bread out of the oven. I would race over and wait (usually impatiently) until the bread came out. Then I would take one of the buns and poke my finger into the middle and wiggle it around to hollow it out a bit. I would then put fresh, real butter and my daddy's homemade blackberry jelly down into the hot bread. It would melt and I would sit and eat that bun with a glass of cold milk. I'm 50 years old and my granny has been gone for nearly 40 years. If I close my eyes and let myself go back in time, I can still smell that wonderful aroma as the bread was baking and still feel my finger burning from sticking it into the bread (you'd think I would have learned to use a knife or fork!!!!) and I can almost taste that wonderful treat. It's one of my most treasured memories of my grandmother, who was my favorite person in the world!"

Introduction

❦

Ahh, salt rising bread. If you have ever taken a bite from a warm slice fresh from the toaster and slathered with butter, you probably remember the moment. Most people do, because salt rising bread makes an impact – no question about it. The baker in the family could be greeted with the smiling faces of children begging for more…or have an aging parent on her deathbed who insists on eating only salt rising bread. Or the baker might be confronted by a spouse who holds his nose and demands that the toast *and* the toaster be put on the back porch immediately. We've seen it all. However, throughout the many generations of families (and in the years that Rising Creek Bakery has been producing and distributing salt rising bread) the reactions are almost universally positive.

It's a bread with a distinctive personality, finicky habits in the baking process, and a marvelous flavor. And it is the object of unabashed nostalgia on the part of people whose memories of a simpler time – perhaps an idealized American past – are intertwined with the taste and smell of salt rising bread.

In many ways this is not your usual bread. The fermentation period for salt rising bread from "starter" to loaf takes a long time – sometimes as long as 24 hours. And then there's the smell! You may have heard it referred to as "stinky bread" (the reason a spouse might hold their nose). We find the pungent smell of the fermented grains to be like a fine cheese. By the time the dough is made, the smell is sweeter. When the loaves are pulled from the oven, the wonderful aroma is of freshly baked bread with a hint of cheese. The seductive aroma of the baked bread has drawn people into homes and bakeries for generations. And by the time it is toasted, well, that is when memories are made. Without a doubt, the smell of salt rising toast has wafted up the stairs of many an old farmhouse, initiating memories that linger for decades.

&

We – Jenny and Susan – have known each other for nearly 25 years, during which time we have shared the wonders, the mysteries, the disappointments and the joys of salt rising bread.

We first met on a cool October evening at a Halloween party at Jenny's rural home. We both had young children then, and a mutual friend had suggested that we should meet. It wasn't long before we realized that we shared a similar interest…salt rising bread! The knowledge had been passed on to us from two remarkable elder bakers – women whom we admired, respected and loved. For Susan, that woman was her grandmother, Katheryn Rippetoe Erwin. For Jenny, it was Pearl Haines, a neighbor of great generosity and heart.

Katheryn Rippetoe Erwin

As grandmothers go, you couldn't beat Katheryn Erwin! [Susan speaking]. She was the best kind of grandmother a child could want. She was funny and wise, gracious and giving, a friend to many, and she loved her grandchildren unconditionally. Like her family for many generations, Grandmother grew up in the southern mountains of West Virginia. She was proud of her West Virginia heritage and instilled in her grandchildren that same fierce pride. She was also proud of her famous salt rising bread. She made it all her life, as did her mother and grandmother.

Katheryn Rippetoe Erwin

I remember well the evenings when Grandmother would carefully place her canning jar, half full with her salt rising bread starter, on top of the pilot light of her gas-heated hot water tank. The tank sat in a small closet in her kitchen, providing just the right temperature needed for the starter to work. The whole family was thrilled when the next morning would greet us with that familiar stinky smell, indicating that we'd all be eating salt rising bread in just a few more hours.

Although I had attempted to make salt rising bread when I was a teenager, it wasn't until I was married and raising a family of my own that I got serious about making this wonderful bread. It was a family tradition that I definitely wanted to carry on. Carefully following one after another of Grandmother's handwritten salt rising bread recipes, I tried and failed and tried again. As I did so, I pictured Grandmother's beautifully gnarled hands making her bread, as I had seen so many times before and, eventually, I got it!

When I'm missing my grandmother and wishing we could sit together once again on her porch swing, I recall a favorite memory of going to her house on Saturday mornings to have breakfast with her. When I arrived at her back door, she would already be making bacon, fried eggs over-easy, and toasted salt rising bread. I remember those days as if they were yesterday, and my heart fills with love, gratitude, and pride…and I miss her even more.

Pearl Haines

Pearl Haines

I *[Jenny]* first met Pearl at Shannon Run Church, down the road from our farmhouse. It was Pearl and her extended family that welcomed us with open arms. We were newcomers to the area, recently arrived from up North with a new baby in tow. The Haineses were our mentors and taught us all kinds of country wisdom that one needs to succeed in a rural setting. I remember one crisp autumn day I drove up the curvy road to their house at the top of the hill and there was Pearl, along with her daughter Martha and daughter-in-law Twyla, out in front of their farmhouse making soap from hog's fat. The three of them were working around a fire with a large kettle on it and steam rising out of the boiling lard. In the background were the steep, deciduous hillsides surrounding them, ablaze with fall colors of red, orange and yellow leaves swirling all around. They graciously allowed me to help in the process.

Later, we shared some delicious food in Pearl's kitchen, and that is where I encountered my first loaf of salt rising bread. I had to ask many questions about this marvelous-tasting bread. As a professionally trained baker, this was the first time I had heard of risen bread made without yeast or without a sourdough starter. I was love-struck in more ways than one. Pearl was so kind as to show me how to make the starter and how to recognize a successful fermentation, and she told a great story, as well. Pearl was an historian in her own right. Her facial expressions, her body movement, and her words helped make the rich but simpler past come alive, in juxtaposition with the modern-day reality in front of us.

12/16/99

I have tried this recipe
— — not have success.
— — able to

Salt Rising Bread

In evening, take 3 tablespoons Cornmeal,
½ tablespoon sugar, ½ tablespoon salt and
½ raw Potato; scrape fine and scald wit
enough water to make quite a thin mus
Set in a warm place until morning.
Combine 1 pint flour, ½ teaspoon salt
And enough lukewarm water to make a
thick batter, then add the mush made
the night before and stir for a minute or
two. Set in warm place. Then light stir

Why are we so enchanted with this delicious bread? Perhaps it is the mystique about it that appeals to us – its puzzling behavior that can try the most patient of bakers' souls. Early American life was filled with mysterious "unknowns." Through religion and superstition, people were able to make sense of such things as the unusual weather, the locust outbursts and childhood diseases. Salt rising bread fit right in with its penchant for unpredictability. In today's world, on the other hand, salt rising's often-frustrating behavior offers a welcome counterpoint to the many aspects of our modern day life that are rote, predictable and endlessly analyzed. As absurd as it sounds, 21st century bakers like ourselves really don't understand much more about how it works and why failures occur than the pioneer women did.

For Jenny, the occasional failures of salt rising bread at Rising Creek Bakery have been by far the hardest aspect of being its proprietor. It is a source of pride to be specializing in authentic salt rising bread and making it available after its long absence. So when a batch of bread fails to work, it is a terrible feeling to disappoint customers – people who may have traveled 50 miles along back roads after working all day, just to buy a loaf.

Yet, we feel deeply that the failures associated with making salt rising bread play an integral role in its appeal. How often does a person get to work through a challenge that is so totally in the hands of nature? We revel in the excitement of discovering how and why salt rising bread works. As bakers, we have discovered that the success of a batch of this bread occurs mostly when we are in tune with the wild microbes and with the earth's rhythms of the seasons. When the dough won't rise, tradition tells us it might be because of the falling barometer or a rushing cold wind outside or the moon pointing down. Or the baker's being pregnant! Now, that is mysterious!

We bring to this book what we have discovered, both in close partnership and as individuals. Susan's perspective is that of a native daughter of Appalachia and the inheritor of a long family tradition of baking salt rising bread – which in many instances became our calling card for gaining the trust of the dozens of elder bakers we interviewed. Our book also benefits from Susan's collection of recipes for salt rising bread, going back to the 18th century. Jenny's perspective is that of a professional baker with deep respect for her craft and a scientist's curiosity and drive to know more (when we write about "the bakery," it is often Jenny's voice you are hearing). And sometimes, one or the other of us will leave a note with her own comment about a topic being discussed. We feel that our combined energies and experiences make this a more complete exploration than either of us might have achieved alone.

Many secrets of salt rising bread are yet to be revealed. In the pages that follow, we attempt to solve some of the mysteries of this nearly lost, very American tradition.

Glossary

Emptins – *"a liquid leavening usually made at home from potatoes or hops and kept from one baking to the next"* (Merriam-Webster)…possibly the first version of a salt rising bread starter

Indian meal (or meal) – the name the Colonial settlers gave to cornmeal

Knead – to work bread dough into a uniform mixture by pressing and folding the dough with your hands

Light dough – dough that has risen and doubled in size

Meal – see Indian meal

Middlings – poor or coarsely-ground flour

Pinch – equal to 1/8 teaspoon

Proofer – a warm, moist chamber where bread dough is placed for the purpose of encouraging the fermentation and rising of the dough

Railroad yeast – An early type of starter. There are different versions in different cookbooks; an early version from the late 1800s uses ginger. Several early 1900s cookbooks describe it as a mixture of cake yeast, potatoes, salt, sugar, and water that is allowed to set overnight or longer. Yet other recipes describe the source as coming from the brewing process.

Raisin' or Risin' or Rising – other names for a salt rising bread starter

Saleratus – a form of potassium or sodium bicarbonate, either manufactured or found naturally on the ground

Scald – to heat to a temperature just short of the boiling point

Warm place – an area or place for raising a starter, sponge or bread dough that is around 104-110°F (40-44°C)

Wild microbes – a mixture of wild yeasts, bacteria and other microscopic organisms naturally found in our environments. When introduced in flour/water mixtures at the right temperature, they reproduce and produce gas to raise the dough, as well as provide flavor profiles to the finished product.

The Three Stages of Salt Rising Bread

❶ Starter – Wild microbes are naturally found in cornmeal, flour and /or potatoes. When these ingredients are mixed with water or milk and heated to a certain temperature, the growth of specific bacteria is promoted. It is these bacteria that produce gas to raise bread, along with the traditional smell and flavor of salt rising bread.

❷ Sponge – a mixture of a fermented starter, flour and water. Its purpose is to coddle the growth of the gas-producing microbes with flour to initiate an increase in volume.

❸ Dough – the sponge, flour, and water mixed together until soft and pliable for shaping into loaves. Its purpose is to create a risen product with delectable flavors.

A Brief History of Salt Rising Bread... and why it matters

The continued interest in discovering our family histories – the people, their stories and the details of the lives they lived – is a powerful testament to the importance of tradition and memory. It grounds us and gives us connection. And one way we connect with our past is through food.

Until not so very long ago, salt rising bread was still being made in American kitchens by women who followed the recipes handed down to them by their mothers and grandmothers, one generation to the next. In many early pioneer homes, salt rising bread was the only bread baked. It was often an essential part of their everyday lives and wellbeing.

And then, for reasons having to do with societal change, a loss of family continuity and the special nature of the bread itself, the tradition of home-baked salt rising bread began to fade. However, through much of the 20th century, salt rising bread could be found in bakeries across the country. In California, for instance – far from Appalachia – the Van de Kamp's bakery chain sold salt rising bread up and down the state until the mid-1970s. Today, Californians of a certain age still remember the salt rising bread from Van de Kamp's

Van de Kamp's Holland Dutch Bakery in Los Angeles, CA, was known for its salt rising bread.

and how good it tasted. How do we know? They're some of Rising Creek Bakery's best customers. They find our bakery online and tell us their stories. And not only Californians. Almost daily, we receive a phone call from someone in a faraway state asking if we really do make it…then asking, with a hopeful voice, "Does it have that salt rising smell?" These are people who remember eating salt rising bread many years before. They tell us how they've yearned to experience again that distinctive taste that carries them back through time, to memories of a cherished youth with extended family gathered around the kitchen table.

For both of us, Susan and Jenny, baking is an integral part of who we are in relation to our lives and our families. In our separate paths to success with making salt rising bread, we each had great curiosity to understand more about it. Even though we had the best of teachers, there were things yet to be discovered. Where did it come from? Who first made it? Why did it sometimes work and other times not? What made its fermentation behave so unpredictably? We joined forces and began looking for answers. One mystery after the next presented itself to us until soon we had quite a list.

Our List of Mysteries

- Where did salt rising bread come from, and who made it first?
- How did salt rising bread get its name when there is little or no salt in its recipes?
- What is happening when a starter does not work?
- What is happening when a sponge does not work?
- What is happening when the loaves do not rise?
- What factors determine the intensity of the "salt rising" aroma?
- What effect does adding ginger to a starter play in the fermentation?
- Why does starter fermentation often not work when the outdoor temperature fluctuates from warm to below freezing?
- What folklore around success or failure can be believed?
- What is it about salt rising bread that makes memories stay alive deep in people's hearts for a lifetime?

Mystery #1

The question that dogged us from the start was where did this absolutely unique bread originate? In our search for its distant beginnings, we have asked hundreds of people to share their traditions of salt rising bread with us, as well as their recipes – from western New York through western Pennsylvania and into the hollows of West Virginia and Kentucky. We researched everything and anything we could get our hands on: scholarly journals, early cookbooks, diaries of pioneer women who described making salt rising bread along the wagon-train trails as they settled in such places as Tennessee, Ohio, Illinois, Michigan, Utah, and, later, California. We contacted food historians, hoping to discover how the bread came to America in the first place, and found only speculation. Even more curious to us is that in extensive travels abroad, wherever we inquired about salt rising bread – in Ireland, Scotland, Germany, and across other continents – we came up empty handed. No one we have encountered seems to know about it outside the United States.

The elusive origins of salt rising bread seem to be centered in and around the Appalachians.

Although the ancestry of many of the pioneers who first settled in the mountains of Appalachia (where salt rising bread was well known) was largely Irish, Scottish and German, there is no evidence to indicate these people brought the knowledge of making salt rising bread from these home countries – nor is there any evidence so far of knowledge about salt rising bread in African slave foodways; the first African American cookbook, from 1881 (*What Mrs. Fisher Knows About Old Southern Cooking*), mentions only yeasted breads.

What we have come to believe, from all the information we have gathered, is that salt rising bread originated because of the dedication and ingenuity of the early pioneer women. In the rugged mountains of Appalachia, these women were isolated, surviving only with what they had on hand. For bread they needed baker's yeast. In the 18th and 19th centuries, the one source for baker's yeast would have been the local brewery. It's likely that these women developed a yeastless bread because beer yeast was either not available for bread-making or not approved of among the many evangelicals living in these mountainous regions.[1]

Could our answer be as simple as that – that these early American women, out of necessity to make a risen bread, discovered that a mixture of flour and water left alone in a warm place would become bubbly after several hours and would work as a leaven for their bread? As J.C. Furnas states (somewhat inelegantly) in his exhaustive historical study, *The Americans: a Social History of the United States*, "salt rising bread evolved by some backwoods housewife possessed of wheat flour but no yeast."

We feel confident in saying that the story of salt rising bread begins in the early pioneer days of Revolutionary-era, pre-industrial United States. The earliest recipe we have found comes from West Virginia in 1778. We have seen other recipes from the 1700s that are very similar to salt rising bread, though not called salt rising, or salt-risin', salt risen or salt-raisin'.

---

1 Reginald Horsman, *Feast or Famine: Food and Drink in American Westward Expansion.* Univ. of Missouri Press. 2008

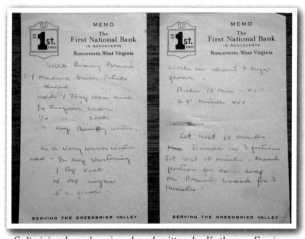

Salt rising bread recipe, handwritten by Katheryn Erwin.

When the original Colonists came to America to start a new life, they brought plant seeds and roots with them from the Old World. They quickly found that the native peoples here had much to show them about indigenous plants never seen outside of this new land, particularly the growing and use of corn – an ingredient, interestingly, that is used in making authentic salt rising bread. Initially, these new plants were not well understood by the Colonists. It would take time and several seasons for them to learn which conditions brought about plentiful produce. And then there was the process of how to incorporate these new foodstuffs into their diet, which led to the creation of new recipes that reflected their European food knowledge and preferences, adapted to this new environment.

Life on the American frontier. The reality of these new pioneers' lives was often harsh, filled with failures, sickness and conflicts with the Native Americans. Yet, by the end of the 1700s, life on the American frontier, including the large region now known as Appalachia, had proven to be a successful and quite bountiful venture. In many ways, the average person during this time lived better than his or her counterpart elsewhere in the world.[2]

There was plenty of meat to hunt, corn and grains to harvest, and squash and beans deliciously prepared to whet the appetites and diversify the daily meals of farmers and their families throughout the seasons.

---

2 David B. Danborn, *Born in the Country.* Johns Hopkins Univ. Press. 1995

The women who originally made salt rising bread were from an era that was very close to nature, organic in all of its composites and daily activities. It was an era when individuals had to be in tune with the world around them for their own safety and survival. These women knew the rhythm of the seasons, their gardens, and the fires they kept. They watched their oven fires closely and were experts at feeding the embers to make a hot fire, or spreading out the glowing cinders to cool the temperature.[3] They also kept close vigil over their doughs, so as not to lose the fermenting microbes or waste valuable ingredients.

The pioneer women who discovered that they could "raise" bread dough without yeast may not have understood how it happened, but they seized the moment and repeated the process until they perfected it. And they shared. The success of this rural life depended on neighborliness and community. Later in the book, we'll see examples of how salt rising starters were shared in these early homes, and into the 20th century. Through hard work and dedication, these women made this well-loved bread for their families and, in so doing, passed on its precious knowledge to future generations.

The Migration Movement of Food. As families outgrew their land space or opportunities, they set their eyes on western horizons. Expansion across the Mississippi began in the early 1800s and continued for the next century. And their food traditions migrated west with them. In the late 1800s and early 1900s, when families had re-assembled after the Civil War, farming and rural living continued to be an esteemed way of life. County fairs were established, celebrating the locally prepared goods. Many farms thrived, benefitting from early mechanization and the burgeoning large-scale agriculture. The farming life seemed to portray what was virtuous about the United States, promising a life of independence as well as security. The men farmed and hunted while the women prepared food and kept a welcoming home. Life was simple, but considered to be noble and good. It was a time that has been seen as defining the American character. A nostalgic time.

---

3 Danborn, ibid.

Rising Bread

1 cup scalded milk
3 Tablespoons sugar
7 Tablespoons white cornmeal
1 teaspoon salt
3 Tablespoons crisco or other shortening
8 cups flour (all purpose)

Combine the hot milk w/
cornmeal and 1 tablespoon sugar
and salt in a (quart size) ?
Mix well. Cover with a cheese
Let stand in a pan of warm
water for 7 or 8 hours til it is
Next step - Mix 2 cups flour w/ ½
warm water - 2 tablespoons sugar
shortening and beat well. ?
in container and place this ?
Pan of warm water til light a
bubbles form.

Mix this with 6 cups o
flour in bowl - Knead well
floured board - shape into about
3 loaves - Let rise til doubled or
longer. Bake 375° for 10 minutes
Reduce temp ? ? ?
25

---

salt + 1½ tea baking power. keep
good and warm until it get real
foaming on top, dip out potatoes
so the liquid add ½ tea baking
Power (thicken to consistency
of soft sponge, and let rise, add
flour to make bread...dough
with flour salt + 2 table sugar
work like yeast bread until dough
is no longer sticky, make out in
loaves and let rise bake 375°
25 to 40 min or until bread (must
keep very warm)

Rising Bread

evening slice 1 med potato into
large mixing bowl add ½ t soda,
3 cups boiling water, ½ t bk powder,
1 T sugar, dash salt (almost as much
salt as sugar) sprinkle ½ c flour evenly
over top

Cool until Lukewarm
Keep warm overnight
Next morning remove potatoes (setting
should be foamy)
Add enough flour about 2 or 3 cups
(about like pancake batter) let rise
until double in size.
White bread is rising
Scald 1 cup milk then add scant ½ cup Crisco
to milk (after removed from heat) add to
the above after it rises 1 T sugar, 1 T salt,
1 t baking powder enough flour to make
loaves
Bake at 350° about 50 min.
            2 loaves.
Loraine Straight

Giulia Ice
208 Summit Drive
Mannington W 26582

---

in Deep Freeze.
Have used this Many
Years I am 83.
★ My Grand Mother
used this same one.
I usualy double and
have 14 to 16 loaves
so I can put
some in Freezer.
Makes good rolls!

Gladys Casdorph
Rt 10 Box 138
Charleston W Va
25312
Tel. 304-343-8990
Wonderful for Bake
Sales.

☙

Our book honors these early pioneer women who persevered out of necessity as they were challenged to feed their families from their surroundings. More than simply a compilation of recipes, baking techniques and serving suggestions, with this book we wanted to capture the voices of people who embody a previously unheralded Appalachian tradition.

In the chapter that follows, you will meet Pearl Haines, as we learn (or attempt to learn) how salt rising bread got its name – the next mystery on our list.

---

4 *William Jasper Henderson and Alvira Aurelia Dickson: a Family History,* by Shelley Dawson Davis, p. 20, 2014

TWO

How the Best Toast in the World Got Its Name

Featuring Pearl Haines of Mount Morris, Pennsylvania

In 1922, at the age of 5, I began making salt raisin' bread in a wooden bowl that my family had been using for generations. My great-grandfather, Thomas Wade, made the bowl in 1869 as a wedding gift for his son's wife. The bowl is still used in the family today to make salt raisin' bread. No one ever washes the bowl, they simply scrape it clean after making the dough. I believe my family had made salt raisin' bread as far back as the 1830s or '40s. The cornmeal-milk recipe that I use was taught to me by my mother, Ethel Fox, born in 1886, who learned it from her mother, Cassie Wade, born in the 1850s. Cassie learned how to make it from her mother, born in 1831. When we could get it, my great-grandmother, grandmother, mother, and myself, all used warm milk directly from the cow.

Pearl Haines in her kitchen with granddaughter Marnie Blake.

In her rambling farmhouse perched crookedly atop the mountain ridge, Pearl Haines intrigues us with the story of her lifelong connection to salt rising bread. Like the majority of people who cherish and love this bread, Pearl's ties to salt rising bread go back many generations. It is typical to find this bread tradition passed down from mother to daughter and from grandmother to granddaughter.

We know that Pearl's great-grandmother was not the only woman baking salt rising bread in the mid-1800s. The yeast that was available then was from beer-making, and commercial yeast was not available in the United States until the 1860s. If a family didn't make beer, or approve of its nature, then the only other options for making raised dough were using pearlash or saleratus. Before we talk more about that, it's important to hear Pearl's words about why she called it salt *raisin'*.

> *You people call it salt risin' bread, but I think it is supposed to be called salt raisin' bread. The sun rises on its own generation, but not bread. If you put a ball of dough on the table, it will just lie there, unless you mix something into it to raise it. Just like a flat tire is raised. That's why we always called it salt raisin' bread. It needs to be raised up by something.*

Pearl tells us this with a distinct air of complete certainty in her voice. Her hands move in front of her as if to say, "Now, you girls listen to me!" Many theories exist about how salt rising bread got its name. With the sincerity that we so admire in Pearl, she explains her theory:

My grandmother used an ingredient in her salt raisin' that was called salt a raitus. I believe that the "salt" in the name salt raisin' bread refers to this ingredient, and it has nothing to do with table salt, as we know it. Way back, people used soda or sody or salt a raitus for various purposes, one of which was to raise dough. This salt a raitus was a mixture of chemicals. In chemists' terms, you mix two or more chemicals together and you have a salt. Same as with baking soda, since it is a mixture, it is also a type of salt. This mixture is a type of salt that raises the bread. That's why I think baking salt raisin' bread was a universal thing back in the early 1800s.

When Pearl speaks of salt a raitus, she is referring to saleratus. Saleratus was used in early recipes of salt rising bread, as well as in biscuits and cakes. It was a manufactured chemical as early as the late 1700s (both as sodium carbonate and potassium carbonate) – but it can also form naturally on the ground, which is often where the pioneer women obtained it in their travels west (see page 40.) It is easy to see how the word salt a raitus evolved from the word saleratus. It is especially easy to see how salt a raitus became "salt rising" – giving us our first theory of how salt rising bread got its name.

Another theory. After salt rising bread became a well-established favorite in Appalachia, the pioneer women took it west with the wagon trains. A second theory about the name's origins has to do with that westward movement, when, out of necessity to find a way to ferment their salt rising bread starter on the trail, women would place it inside the salt barrel on the wagon wheel, to hold it in a warm place (in the sunshine) by day. In the evening, after the starter had time to rise using the heat-keeping property of the salt in the salt barrel, the women baked their salt rising bread in Dutch ovens around the campfire.

SALT RISING BREAD AND DUTCH OVENS
ON THE OREGON TRAIL

Thomas E. Cooley, born in 1872, describes how salt rising bread was made in his youth (in a 1956 interview with Velma Olling):

The cabin in which I first lived had neither cook stove nor heating stove, but a fireplace serving for both. A tin reflector about 30 inches long was used for baking. The pans filled with salt-rising bread were pushed into the bottom of it and baked in the direct heat from the open fireplace. Dutch ovens were used around the campfire on the trip across the plains, to bake bread.

Just before we leave the mountaintop, Pearl tempts us to have some of her warm salt raisin' bread:

> My family ate salt raisin' bread hot from the oven with a thick layer of butter on it. We also toasted it on a wood fire, sometimes purposely dropping it in the ashes, or steamed it over a kettle of boiling water, which we called smoked bread. By far, however, our favorite way to eat salt raisin' bread was to place a fresh slice on a pie plate, pour coffee over the slice, sprinkle it with brown sugar, and then pour real cow's cream, thick and sweet, over it all.

Like Pearl's family, other lovers of salt rising bread describe their favorite way of eating this memorable bread, and most often it is as toast. In a survey of a hundred customers at the Rising Creek Bakery, we found that the overwhelming majority prefer to eat their salt rising bread toasted with butter. Another favorite way to eat it is as grilled cheese sandwiches, or as a fresh tomato-cucumber sandwich. Others enjoy their salt rising bread with coffee and sugar poured over it, while some like to eat it sliced with gravy on top.

Pearl is gone now. We will never forget her, and we will be forever grateful for the many hours we sat in her home while she so willingly and proudly answered every question we could possibly ask her about salt rising bread. She taught us so much!

Today, the Haines generations who have come after Pearl are still carrying on this family tradition. Pearl made sure that she taught her daughters and granddaughters to make salt rising bread, and one of Pearl's great-grandchildren is now making salt rising bread in the same wooden bowl made in 1869. Here is the recipe that the family still uses today and that Pearl lovingly passed on to so many people who continue to help keep this tradition alive.

❥ PEARL HAINES'S SALT RISING BREAD RECIPE ❧

INGREDIENTS

½ cup scalded milk

3 tsp. cornmeal

1 tsp. flour

⅛ tsp. baking soda

PREPARATION

1. Pour milk onto the dry ingredients and stir.

2. Keep warm overnight until foamy.

3. After the raisin' has foamed and has a rotten cheese smell, in a medium-sized bowl add 2 cups of warm water to mixture, then enough flour (about 1½ cups) to make like a thin pancake batter. Stir and allow to rise again until it becomes foamy. This usually takes about 2 hours.

4. Next, add 1 cup of warm water for each loaf of bread you want to make, up to 6 loaves (e.g., 6 cups of water makes 6 loaves of bread). Add enough flour (20 cups for 6 loaves or about one 5 pound bag of flour plus ⅓ bag of flour). Form into loaves and grease tops. Let loaves rise in greased pans for 1.5 to 3 hours – sometimes longer if it is a cold day.

5. Bake at 350° F (180° C) for 35 to 45 minutes or until loaves sound hollow when tapped.

Two Salt Rising Bread Memories, Sent to Susan's Salt Rising Bread Project

I grew up eating salt risin' bread! My grandma (Dad's mom) made it, and after my parents married, my mom learned how to make it. I love it! My mom found someone who makes it—not bad, but it's not my grandma's. We ate it for breakfast and called it "bread and coffee." We soaked the bread with coffee, poured milk and sugar on it and then a slice of cheese. I can still smell it in my grandma's house— great memories!

[No state given]

❧

I am ninety years old and have very fond memories of salt risen bread. As a preteen, I spent most of my summers with my widowed grandmother and her niece on the farm. Thursday was baking day and Wednesday night "cousin Mag" prepared the starter from I don't know what except there was a potato and meal and possibly some milk. The meal was our own having been ground by a local mill from our corn. The starter was placed in the warming oven of an old wood burning stove. How they kept the temperature up during the night, I don't know, but it worked. Thursday the baking began, and we had fresh bread with homemade butter and homemade jam that day and for a few days longer.

[from Richmond, Kentucky]

How Can Something Smell So Bad, But Taste So Good?

a tale of friendly bacteria, baking failures and science, too

Featuring Janice Bromage of Fairview, West Virginia

Marie Jones of Core, West Virginia

Della Mae Tennant of Wadestown, West Virginia

Early one morning, in the small West Virginia village of Fairview, Janice Bromage was mixing her salt rising bread starter into a bowl. The starter had been fermenting all night and was nice and foamy. Janice certainly noted the strong smell of the starter as she added flour and water to make her sponge and knew this was a good sign! The smell is an indicator that the fermentation is working as it should. Her son woke up and walked into the kitchen: "Mom, how can something smell so bad, but taste so good?"

Many people have asked the same question over the years.

We knew the answer involved the behavior of bacteria. But how? In an attempt to solve this mystery, we sent salt rising bread cornmeal starter samples to a scientific laboratory in Minnesota, R-Tech Laboratories, in order to see what the microbial contents were. The results that came back were fascinating. Instead of yeast, salt-rising starters use common bacteria derived from the cornmeal and/or potatoes. These microbes appear to be a symbiotic mixture of wild bacterial species that are ubiquitous in the environment, present on most grains and found in the healthy microflora of our own guts.

How is it possible to create a food product that starts out smelling bad but results in something so delicious as to even cause nostalgia on one's deathbed? Any microbiologist knows that when rotting food smells foul, typically, the rotting is caused by some bacterium. Many cheeses are fermented by bacteria, such as Brie, cheddar, and Parmesan. The initial steps of cheese-making produce strong, slightly unpleasant odors due to these proprietary bacterial blends. The odor of the fermentations responsible for altering the milk and resulting in a solid mass are vastly different from the smell of the final product. When the fermented cheese is ready, the resulting taste is thoroughly enjoyed for its wonderful, delicate and complex flavors. It is the same with salt rising bread. As James Furnas observed about salt rising bread in his book, *The Americans: a Social History of the United States*: "Indeed it is, when at its best, as if a delicately reared, unsweetened plain cake had had an affair with a Pont l'Eveque cheese."

Enhancing the Smell in Salt Rising Bread

Over the years, we have learned so much from the bread-baking elders of this region of Appalachia, who have helped us unlock the mysteries of our favorite bread. This one has to do with replacing the salt – the type of salt you use in your starter – with baking soda.

One ingredient that is often used in salt rising bread starters is some type of salt. The salt can be common table salt (NaCl) or it can be a type of chemical salt, such as baking soda or saleratus (see glossary and page 40). We have Marie Jones to thank for telling us about the smell-enhancing qualities of baking soda.

Marie Jones

The bakery had been in existence for three years when we visited Marie Jones in Core, West Virginia. It was a cold December day, a couple of weeks before Christmas. Marie was in her nineties then and lived down a rural dirt road in the same house where she was born. We had to drive slowly to avoid skidding on the ice and gingerly made our way up her steep driveway to the front door. We hadn't met her previously, but we had heard numerous accolades from customers at the bakery about her generosity, as well as her delicious salt rising bread. Marie made us feel at home right away with her warm, blue eyes and quiet, sincere words of welcome. The cozy home was decorated for the holidays, including a small Christmas tree. Marie made loving sacrifices for many people throughout her life. Although she recently passed away, her family and friends will long remember her and her endless kindness to them all.

Marie Jones

Marie had been baking salt rising bread most of her life, as she reminisces here:

Early of a morning, I'd begin my starter with potatoes, cornmeal, sugar and baking soda. I'd work all day as a janitor in the local school, then come home and smell my starter. If it was strong smelling and foamy, then I'd begin making my salt rising bread.

Now, as soon as someone mentions a strong smelling starter, our ears perk up. A strong smell is what you want with your starter, as that is an indication of a successful fermentation, which means your dough will likely rise. We told Marie that many people had commented to us that the salt rising bread from the bakery didn't have a strong enough smell. She asked us what we used in our starter recipe, and when we mentioned salt, she suggested we try baking soda instead, because it will help increase the smell. She was right! Now we always use baking soda in our starter at the bakery. Since then, we have not heard comments from our customers about our bread not being smelly enough. Of course, "smelliness" will always be a subjective thing.

Successful salt rising bread starter

Della Mae Tennant

Della Mae Tennant, from Wadestown, West Virginia, has been making salt rising bread for decades. We visited her in her farmhouse in the late summer. Because she is a widow and lives alone now, she doesn't bake as much as she used to. But she is happy to impart her salt rising bread knowledge – starting with how her family feels about the smell:

Della Mae Tennant

> *I can't remember if my husband liked it, as he has been dead for 37 years. All the kids like it. I got two son-in-laws who hate it. One daughter can't make it in her house because her husband can't stand the smell and the other don't even like to smell it toastin' in the toaster. She and her girlfriend make it at her girlfriend's house.*

Here is Della Mae's recipe, which she generously shared with us:

> *For my starter, I put in a jar: 2 potatoes, 2 tablespoons of sugar, 2 tablespoons of cornmeal, and a pinch of soda. Then, I cover it all with 2 cups of boiling water. I set my bowl in my oven where I have a 75-watt bulb. It keeps it at just the right temperature and it takes from 10 to 12 hours. I usually set mine about 5 in the evening then it'll be ready early in the morning. If it doesn't have a good foam on it and it don't stink, then it won't make good bread. Oh, yes. I've had failures. Some mornings you get up and there's nothing.*

The Puzzling Question of Failures

We continued to research salt rising bread because failures continued to occur, even though we made it regularly. Failures can occur throughout the starter stage, the sponge stage or the dough stage. At times, the failures seem to be due to weather, low barometric pressure, or a change in the ingredients. For example, the starter may never develop a foamy top. Or the starter might work beautifully, but the sponge doesn't double in size. At times, the sponge rises well, but the loaves take hours to rise, if they even rise at all. One has to expect such variance with wild bacteria. The genetic variation of one batch of wild microbes captured in a starter may contain genes that have weak rising power but strong smells. The following week, the batch of microbes may contain genes with strong rising power but no smell.

In 1912, Winona Woodward, an ambitious woman whose curiosity and drive led her to complete a master's of science, devoted her studies to the failures of salt rising bread. In her master's thesis at the University of Missouri, Ms. Woodward's research described how temperature and bacterial cultures play a major role in the success of salt rising bread. Her research was on the horizon of microbial understanding because in 1912 there was no knowledge of genes, DNA, or nuclei in cells. This insight led her to draw valid conclusions from sound scientific design and reasoning. She concluded that one set of bacteria existed in cornmeal to produce the wonderful flavor of salt rising bread and that a different bacteria produced enough gas to raise the bread (validating Pearl Haines's reasoning that this bread should be called *salt raisin'*). Amazingly, one hundred years later, scientists still do not fully understand the complex microbial interactions in salt rising bread.

Because this bread tastes so good and is so temperamental, throughout its history others have been propelled to find answers to salt rising bread's failures.

In 1909, the governor of Kansas, Walter Stubbs, who loved salt rising bread, spoke enthusiastically about it in his campaign speeches. He swore that his strength and

endurance were due to his consuming salt rising bread three times a day. He felt that a revolution in bread making had occurred, since yeast was not an ingredient when making salt rising bread. After he was elected, Governor Stubbs funded a laboratory at the University of Kansas headed by a young scientist, Dr. Henry Kohman. Stubbs told his constituents that Dr. Kohman would be able to eliminate failures surrounding salt rising bread and offer solutions to all the housewives who were having trouble with their salt rising bread. After just a few years, Kohman did just that. From 1916 to 1995 (an impressive 70+ years!), Kohman's Salt Rising Yeast sold to commercial bakeries, and then to home bakers through King Arthur Flour Company. In Chapter 7 you will find more about how Kohman's patents helped bring about the large-scale commercialization of salt rising bread. When production of the salt rising yeast ended in 1995 and bakeries ran out of it, the commercial production of salt rising bread came to a halt. Bakers had grown so dependent on this product that they had forgotten how to make the original recipe!

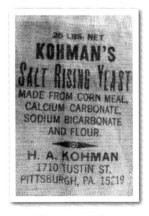

At Rising Creek Bakery, the demise of the salt rising bread yeast has been to our benefit. Having lost their favorite commercial sources for salt rising bread, people all over the United States still want it – and now they can search online to find it. We are one of the few bakeries that produce salt rising bread using the authentic recipe, without the addition of commercial yeast. We now expect failures to happen only about three or four times a year. Yes, revenue is lost, but we remain true to the nature of salt rising bread made without commercial yeast, to preserve its marvelous authentic flavor and texture. We are also one of just a handful of bakeries that ship the bread throughout the United States, thus satisfying the

taste buds and memories of thousands of people who grew up with this wonderful bread and toast.

We have to be constantly observant of any minute changes in the three stages of preparation because as the seasons change and temperatures fluctuate, so does the making of salt rising bread (one of the vexing mysteries on our Mysteries list). We have learned to have nerves of steel; when a failure occurs, it often catches us off guard. A week or two before Thanksgiving is often when the failures begin. One Christmas season, we had two weeks of failures. More than one hopeful customer walked out of the bakery in tears.

The persistence of failures, along with basic human curiosity, has driven us to keep asking why. Could one reason be the chemicals sprayed on potatoes that prevent them from sprouting? It seems reasonable to think that such chemicals could stop the bacteria from growing, and hence no foamy starters. (We have tried organic potatoes and found them to work well.) But there are more variables than just that.

Humans... After decades of making this bread, we believe that one recurring reason for failures in the creation of salt rising bread is the baker's inattentiveness to what is going on as a batch develops. There is a small window when each stage is ready that the baker must be familiar with to ensure a successful batch. If the baker is not present during the limited time period when a starter is ready, failure can occur: If the potatoes (and/or cornmeal) are too old, the starter may not ferment properly. Additionally, if the potatoes have green on them, sometimes the starter will not work. Likewise, if the temperature of the starter is a few degrees too low or too high, the fermentation will be unsuccessful. These examples suggest that whoever is making the bread must be ever-present and watchful during the critical parts of the process, in case adjustments must be made.

If there is a salt rising bread baker's mantra, it is the one Pearl Haines always said:

> **"YOU MUST PAY ATTENTION, AND YOU CANNOT HURRY IT ALONG."**

The Effect of Outside Temperature

[Jenny] At the bakery, we find that when the outside temperature fluctuates from above to below freezing, the salt rising starter doesn't work well. On one of those days, Susan was also making starters at her home (she lives a mile from the bakery on top of a hill)…and her starters worked. This is a mystery that I don't have a clue about.

Investigating the Bacteria

An interesting bacterial species found in salt rising bread is *Clostridium perfringens*. *Clostridium* is found everywhere in nature, including the human gut where it is a part of the healthy microflora. But because strains of this bacteria can also cause enteritis (stomach cramping with diarrhea) and because at the time we were making this bread regularly for our children and spouses, we wanted to understand more about it. Luckily for us, Dr. Bruce McClane, a world-renowned microbiologist and expert on *Clostridium perfringens*, was just an hour's drive north of where we live.

We drove to the University of Pittsburgh with a dozen salt rising bread starters and several loaves of bread to meet Dr. McClane and his graduate assistants. They cultured our samples, found lots of *Clostridium*, but found none of the molecules that can cause enteritis. They investigated further to examine the DNA of the bacteria in the salt rising samples and did not even find the genes that could produce the diarrhea-producing toxin that causes enteritis. This was wonderful news! McClane's scientists did find a few bacterial spores in the baked bread, indicating that some bacteria can survive the baking process, but these numbers were so low that there is no need to be concerned. Still, there are some people for whom even the mention of bacteria in their food is cause for alarm. Our prediction is that in the near future, with the current advances in human microflora research, microbiologists and nutritionists will gain insight into the important role of

bacteria in the gut and how our microflora keep us healthy. Then salt rising bread will become known as a food that promotes healthy digestion – perhaps confirming one of the long-standing traditional beliefs about the bread, that it calms the stomach like a good cup of chamomile tea.

In 2008, we co-authored an article in the *West Virginia Medical Journal* with Dr. Greg Juckett stating McClane's results. It is reassuring to know that nowhere in the history of salt rising bread is there any evidence of anyone feeling discomfort or getting sick from eating this bread.

Our meeting with Dr. McClane led to an opportunity for us to write a chapter in the scientific textbook *Handbook of Indigenous Foods Involving Alkaline Fermentation*. Interestingly for us, while preparing our manuscript, we learned about two breads that use a similar fermentation process as salt rising bread. One is from northern Greece and uses chickpeas in the starter. The other bread (called *gergoush*) is from the Sudan and uses lentils and milk in the starter. Both the Greek bread and the Sudanese bread have been researched extensively in order to understand the symbiotic role of bacteria in the fermentation of these bread starters. We speculate that the bacterial relationships are the same for salt rising bread. More research is needed. A thorough scientific investigation of the microbes in salt rising bread would confirm these findings. How do these bacteria interact with each other? Which microbe produces the wonderful flavor and which one the memorable smell? Which one causes the bread to rise? Is there any truth to the long-held belief that eating the bread calms the stomach? Last, but not least, why do failures occur during the starter and sponge process? We are still in pursuit of answers. We invite individuals to conduct sound scientific investigations about salt rising bread to help solve these and other mysteries of this bread.

⑤ SALT RISING BREAD TOAST ⑥

INGREDIENTS

Salt rising bread
Butter
Homemade jam or apple butter

PREPARATION

1. Slice salt rising bread according to your preference of thickness.

2. Place slices in the toaster and begin toasting. When making salt rising toast, you must set your toaster on medium to high heat and toast for a longer period of time to get a nice golden brown color. Yeasted bread generally has a higher sugar content due to alcohol fermentation, whereas salt rising bread's bacterial fermentation forms less sugar, thus the need for its longer toasting time.

3. Slather with butter and add homemade jam or apple butter, if preferred.

EGGS WITH TOAST

INGREDIENTS

Salt rising bread
2 farm fresh eggs
Butter
Salt and pepper, to taste

PREPARATION

1. Fry fresh eggs in a frying pan according to your liking.
2. Toast slices of bread (as above).
3. Slather with butter and place the eggs and toast on a plate to enjoy.

GRILLED CHEESE SANDWICH

INGREDIENTS

2 slices of salt rising bread
Butter for covering bread
   and grilling sandwich
2-3 pieces of good cheese
Mayonnaise, if desired

PREPARATION

1. Butter one side of each slice of bread.

2. Put 2-3 slices of good cheese between 2 slices of salt rising bread.

3. Grill in frying pan on stove until bread is golden and cheese is melted, about 5 minutes.

FOUR

The Staff of Life: How Bread Made Its Way into Our Hearts and Hearths

꙰

Bread has been a central part of human cultures since before any seeds were sown by human hands. Tens of thousands of years ago, when hunter-gatherers were foraging, humans gathered the seed heads of emmer, wheat, barley, corn, peas and beans. These wild seeds were threshed and hulled, then ground between stones. Moving forward in time, we see early pictographs showing women bent over a flat rock, grinding with an oblong stone in their hands.

Archeological evidence for the widespread consumption of grains comes from ancient Mesoamerican, Egyptian and early Greek times. It reveals the presence of flatbreads as well as risen breads. Flatbreads (tortillas) from the Aztec culture in Mexico were prepared by boiling grains in lye made from ashes to improve their flavor and digestibility. Flatbreads from ancient Greece, along with the risen breads in ancient Egypt, were prepared using spontaneous fermentations composed of wild bacteria and yeast.

Pictured above is a metate, a stone tool used for grinding grains and seeds.

Which Came First, Bread or Beer?

Similar microbes are used to ferment beer and bread. Since microbes have inhabited the earth far longer than humans, these living creatures have always been available for humans to tinker with. One can imagine that early cultures enjoyed getting away from routine daily meals, as much as we do now, by enhancing their food flavors through purposeful fermentation. Take, for example, the early Egyptian culture and how they were known to enjoy fermented beverages (evidence of yeast for brewing and leavening comes from as early as 6,000 years ago). And in ancient Mesopotamia, there is a 4,000-year-old Sumerian tablet that records a receipt for "best" beer from a brewer named Alulu. So, had fermented alcoholic beverages been discovered prior to bread-making, or did bread come first – or did they evolve together? We don't yet know.

Ancient Sumerian tablet beer receipt

Think back about food preparation thousands of years ago. Imagine a forgotten pot of grains soaking in water on a warm summer night. As the grains are ripe with invisible wild microbes and the temperature is ideal, the mixture spontaneously ferments. These billions of microbes have altered the flavor adding new levels of complexity to the grains, perhaps adding a slightly "cheesy" flavor or perhaps making the grains taste a bit sour. Now envision the next morning, when an early riser sticks a finger in this brew to smell and taste it. What immediate pleasure is found! Perhaps this person is moved to share this new and tasty concoction with others for a meal or as a beverage. Eventually, people figure out how to replicate and nurture the fermented brew so it can be used over and over. Fame spreads across hillsides and cities, demand for it grows, and the fermented food product becomes established as bread and/or beer.

This is how we think that naturally fermented breads may have developed over time. Alas, as the crumbs have long disintegrated, there are no actual remains of any foods or prepared dough from 5,000 years ago to lead us to a point of origin, so we must piece

Fermented sponge, opposite

history together in other ways. Archeological digs have unearthed clusters of blackened stones from thousands of years back that suggest early ovens. This points to the origin of baking and the beginning of how complex food preparations evolved over time. Through augmented skills of cooking and fermentation methods passed down through the millennia, our human ancestors acquired rich traditional foodways that brought much nourishment and pleasure to daily living and through sharing with others. These traditions have led to evocative memories associated with food and family.

Salt Rising Bread's Early Recipes

There is evidence that salt rising bread was being made as early as the late 18th century in America; in a modern collection of recipes from Lewisburg, West Virginia, we found one salt rising bread recipe dated 1778, as we mentioned in the introduction.

Salt Risen Bread • 1778

At night: Bring 1 cup sweet milk just to a scald, stir in enough meal [cornmeal] to make a soft mush, and keep warm until morning.

If not light in the morning, stir and set in a bowl of warm water until it is light.

Whenever mush is light, thicken 1 cup lukewarm water to a stiff batter with flour, stir into a mush and set in a bowl of warm water to double in bulk.

Then mix in 2½ cups warm water, 2 tablespoons sugar, 2 teaspoons salt, ½ cup melted lard, flour to make a medium dough.

Knead vigorously. Put down in three loaves. Allow to rise in a warm place.

Bake in a moderate oven for about an hour.

~ From The Greenbrier P.E.O. Cookbook, 1978

Recipe handed down in the family of Rena Scott, who contributed it to the collection.

Note: It is common for recipes to alter somewhat in their wording as they are passed down from generation to generation. This recipe is an example of that. In 1778, a baker would not have been making bread in a "moderate oven" since it wasn't until the late 1800s that wood-fired ranges were invented for cooking and baking. Before that time, cooking was done in the open hearth with large lidded pots, such as Dutch ovens, hanging over the coals. But what suggests to us that this recipe is from that period is the use of such period words as "sweet milk" (fresh from the cow), "meal" (for cornmeal) and, especially, "light" ("if not light in the morning"). See the use of "light" in the recipe below.

Receipt for Making Excellent Bread Without Yeast • 1833

Scald about two hands full of Indian meal, into which put a little salt and as much cold water as will make it rather warmer than new milk; then stir in wheat flour, till it is as thick as a family pudding, and set it down by the fire to rise. In about half an hour it generally grows thin; you may sprinkle a little fresh flour on the top, and mind to turn the pot round that it may not take to the side of it. In three or four hours, if you mind the above directions, it will rise and ferment as if you had set it with hop yeast; when it does, make it up in soft dough, flour a pan, put in your bread, set it before the fire, covered up, turn it round to make it equally warm, and in about half an hour it will be light enough to bake. It suits best to bake in a Dutch oven as it should be put into the oven as soon as it is light.

~ From Mrs. Lydia Child's The American Frugal Housewife, *1833, 12th edition, enlarged and corrected by the author.*

Emptins: the original salt rising bread starters?

The first cookbook from early America (*First American Cookery*, Amelia Simmons, 1796), mentions the use of emptins to raise rusk, which is what early breads were called. (Rusk consisted of dry-baked doughs that would last because there wasn't even enough moisture in the bread for molds to grow!) Here is a recipe from Amelia Simmons's cookbook, calling for emptins:

> Take an earthen vessel that you then scald, add water as hot as your finger can stand, then place in salt, sugar, flour, and sometimes pearlash or sometimes emptins. Within 5 hours it should rise.

Amelia Simmons's recipe calls for additional flour to make into dough once it has risen well. It was then baked.

Emptins is a *liquid leavening usually made at home from potatoes or hops and kept from one baking to the next* [Merriam-Webster]. The use of emptins originated in the ancient world, as far back as Egypt. Emptins was a mixture of wild bacteria and yeast (whereas today's sourdoughs and beer brews have been perfected to utilize just yeast alone – *Saccharomyces cerevisiae*). Bakers would add handfuls of the bacteria-yeast-laden emptins into their breads, cakes and biscuits as a leavener. There is evidence of women sharing starters or emptins to make salt rising bread and calling it emptin bread. Keep in mind that these emptins varied extensively from house to house and from day to day. Since the concentration and types of microbes within each batch were unique, there was lots of guesswork, resulting in inconsistent breads. It could be that these emptins were the original salt rising bread starters.

How is Salt Rising Bread Different from Sourdough Bread?

Is there a difference between salt rising bread and sourdough? That is a question we are often asked, and it's an interesting one because both breads utilize the wild microbes on the grains to make a starter. Below are three key differences:

1. *Fermentation temperature:* Salt rising bread needs a very warm environment (104-110° F, 40-44°C) for fermentation, which encourages the wild bacteria to reproduce. Sourdough fermentation, on the other hand, occurs at room temperature (65-75° F, 18-25°C), which encourages the wild yeasts to reproduce. The difference in these temperatures and in the resulting bacteria vs. yeast proliferation accounts for the difference in the resulting taste and smell of the two breads.

2. *The starter's lifespan:* The starter that is used in sourdough bread can be kept for years by periodically replenishing it with flour. The starter that is used in salt rising bread must be used immediately. (On page 59, we discuss ways that a salt rising bread starter can be frozen or dried for future use – though not reliably. So the rule of thumb is that it is to be used as soon as it is ready. Still, it's good to know that there are options you can experiment with for yourself.)

3. *Texture:* Salt rising bread has a dense, close crumb, while sourdough bread is light and airy. The primary gas that raises the bread in salt rising is hydrogen, and in sourdough it is carbon dioxide. It is this difference in gas, and perhaps in the amount of gas produced, that affects the crumb, along with salt rising's tendency to have a flat top. In addition, the crust of salt rising bread is very thin, and the crust of sourdough bread is typically more robust– sometimes described as crispy or crackling.

Other Leaveners – from Pearlash to Saleratus

In the early 1800s, the first descriptive use of leaveners other than ale-yeast appears in American cookbooks: pearlash was added to gingerbreads and biscuits. This compound (sometimes referred to as salt of tartar or the less-refined potash) is a powdery abrasive residue left over from wood fires. The use of pearlash in American cooking may have been

learned from the European forebears, who had known of it for centuries as a byproduct from glassmaking. It is regarded as a type of salt, alkaline in nature, and when added to dough mixtures promotes the release of CO_2, causing the dough to rise. But it wasn't until a few decades later that pearlash was included in recipes for breadmaking.

By the mid to late 1800s, European forests were being depleted and industrialization was beginning to take off – so with pearlash in high demand, chemically derived products replaced it. This imported product was called saleratus (from the Latin for aerated salt), derived from common salt, sulfuric acid, coal, and limestone. Soon American entrepreneurs began producing their own brand of saleratus, whereupon pearlash fell out of favor.

Women on the westward trails often gathered their own natural saleratus when they found it, utilizing this substance to raise their biscuits and breads, including salt rising bread.

> **In order to make their bread and cakes rise, the emigrants [westward-bound pioneers] carefully packed saleratus for their travel. If the supply of saleratus brought from home was depleted, the emigrants supplemented it from natural soda springs found in Wyoming and Utah.** (*On the Frontier: Minnesota Cooking from 1850 to 1900*, Marjorie Kreidberg)

Through much of the 19th century, most baking was still done over an open fire, which didn't lend itself to consistent, high quality baked goods. Relief came in the 1870s, when wood-burning ranges became fixtures in most homes. With the better ovens and commercial saleratus, the quality of baked goods was more consistent, resulting in increased varieties of baked products and increased demand.

As European trends and traditions in bread were established with each new wave of immigrants arriving, the demand for baked goods remained high. By the early 1900s, yeast

as we know it today was used in breads, while saleratus and baking soda were used in quick-breads, other pastries, and salt rising bread.

Here is a salt rising bread recipe that uses saleratus, probably from the end of the 19th century. It also uses ginger, which is unusual. It is from *Recipes From the Mountains*, published by The Relief Society of the Church of Jesus Christ of Latter-Day Saints, Beckley, West Virginia. Though there is no date on the cookbook, all the recipes are over 100 years old.

> In the morning, while getting breakfast, set your rising for the day's baking as follows: Put into a 2 qt. pitcher, 1 and 1/2 pints of hot water, a very small teaspoonful of salera-tus, and not quite so much salt, and twice the quantity of ginger as saleratus. Let this stand until lukewarm and then stir in enough flour to thicken quite thick. Set the pitcher in water heated as hot as you can bear your hands in. Keep the water about the same temperature until the rising is ready to run over the top of the pitcher, then make the bread thus. Sift into the bread pan the quantity of flour that you intend baking. Make a hole in the middle of the flour and pour in your rising and enough flour to make a stiff dough. Grease baking tins and divide the lump of dough into loaves. Knead them until as smooth as glass. Grease the top of the loaf with a little butter and set in a warm place to rise. More heat is required to raise this bread than hop yeast but less wood will bake it. I make my bread in this manner often (for 2 years) without my rising once failing in coming.

The popularity of salt rising bread kept up with yeasted breads, due in large part to salt rising's wonderful flavor. But failures continued to plague bakers. In an 1885 issue of *The Ohio Farmer*, a housewife inquired about which brand of flour made the best salt rising bread with the fewest failures. Another housewife inquired of millers about a difference in flours for yeasted versus salt rising and how they are ground, because the new process of

grinding flour for yeasted breads did not seem to produce flour that worked well for salt rising bread.

Those with baking knowledge pointed out that bakers who made good yeasted bread will have problems once they try to make salt rising bread, as the process is different in several ways: First, yeasted breads are kept at a lower temperature during the bread-making process; with salt rising bread, the temperature is significantly higher throughout all stages. Second, salt rising bread requires less kneading than yeasted breads. Third, salt rising bread requires less flour than yeasted breads.

Transitioning between the two methods presents challenges today as it did then, but a good baker can contend with such variances. It's like making two types of pastries – one method is just different from another. Despite these hindrances, many people still wanted their salt rising bread. An example can be seen in an article in *The New York Times*, September 15, 1889, which tells of a near-riot of home bakers at a recent Ohio fair:

"Housewives at War"

The biggest premium at the Manchester Fair last week was $15 for the best loaf of salt-rising bread and it stirred up a big row. Nearly every woman in Adams County and many from adjoining counties who were at all versed in the culinary art must have tried for that blue ribbon, as there were loaves upon loaves piled up… After the premium was awarded it was discovered that one of the judges was related to the successful exhibitor, and of course this created a big racket. New judges had to be selected, and the ribbon was tied the second time. The unsuccessful exhibitors did not quiet down, however. They declared the judges 'didn't know anything about bread, nohow!' More than 100 families are at swords' points, and at least one engagement has been declared off. Scarcely a day passes without a fight, and the whole county is worked up over the affair.

Toast-Making in a Simpler Time

Almost everyone who loves salt rising bread says that eating it toasted with butter is their favorite way to enjoy it. That's been the case for a very long time. Before the invention of the electric toaster, bread was toasted over an open fire, and a young housewife in the 19th century might appreciate some guidance on how best to do it. Here is toast wisdom from *Miss Leslie's Directions for Cookery*, written in 1851:

> Cut the bread in even slices and moderately thick. When cut too thin, toast is hard and tasteless. It is much nicer when the crust is pared off before toasting. A long-handled toasting fork (to be obtained at the hardware or tin stores) is far better than the usual toasting apparatus made to stand before the fire and the slices of bread slipped in between and, therefore, liable to be browned in stripes, dark and light alternately; unless the bread while toasting is carefully slipped along so that the whole may receive equal benefit from the fire. With a fork whose handle is a yard in length, the cook can sit at a comfortable distance from the fire, and the bread will be equally browned all over; when one side is done, taking it off the fork and turning the other.

What is it about toast that people love so much? Does the smoky, burned taste remind us of sitting in front of long-ago fires? Nostalgia aside, toasting, as a process of browning, can enhance flavors, and create a more secure platform for toppings, such as butter and jam.

The first electrical toaster was invented by Alan MacMaster from Scotland in the 1890s. But it was an American, Charles Strite, who invented the pop-up toaster in 1919.

It has been more than 6,000 years since we humans started our love affair with bread, and there's no sign of its letting up anytime soon! We're closing this chapter with Susan's grandmother's recipe for salt rising bread. This classic recipe has drawn generations of Susan's family into the kitchen for a slice – or maybe two – of the best toast in the world.

⊚ KATHERYN RIPPETOE ERWIN'S SALT RISING BREAD ℮

This is a standard salt rising bread recipe, using potatoes and water in the starter.

INGREDIENTS

1 medium Irish potato, sliced and placed in a jar

ADD

1 tablespoon cornmeal   **¼ tsp. salt**
¼ tsp. soda   **2 cups boiling water**

PREPARATION

1. Cover and let rise in a warm place until morning. (I set mine on top of the pilot light on my hot water tank). If the mixture is foamy and has the salt rising bread "aroma" the next morning, pour off the liquid and throw away the potatoes.
2. Mix 2 cups of very warm water with ½ cup of shortening. Then add 1 teaspoon salt, 4 teaspoons sugar, and 5 cups flour. Combine with rising mixture (starter) to make a stiff batter. Let this rise until double in bulk.
3. Work in 6 cups of flour, to make a soft dough. Divide into 3 portions. Let rise 10 minutes. Knead for 3 minutes. Place in 3 greased pans. Let rest until dough reaches the top of the pan.
4. Bake at 450°F (230°C) for 15 minutes, then at 400°F (200°C) for 25 minutes.

⑨ SALT RISING BREAD STUFFING ℮

INGREDIENTS

16 cups of 1-inch salt rising bread
    cubes (1½# loaf)
8 T (1 stick) unsalted butter
2 cups medium diced onion (2 onions)
1 cup medium diced celery (2 stalks)
2 T chopped, fresh parsley or 2 tsp.
    dried parsley
1 T salt
1 tsp. black pepper
1-2 cups turkey broth or chicken stock

PREPARATION

1. Preheat oven to 350°F (180°C)

2. Place the bread cubes in a single
   layer on a sheet pan and bake for
   7 minutes.

3. Remove the bread cubes to a very large bowl.

4. Melt the butter and add the onions, celery, parsley, salt, and pepper. Cook over medium heat for
   10 minutes until the vegetables are softened. Add to the bread cubes.

5. Add the turkey (or chicken) broth or stock to the mixture. Mix well and pour into a greased
   9x12-inch baking dish.

6. Bake, uncovered, for 30 minutes, until browned on top and hot in the middle. Serve warm.

INGREDIENTS

8 T (1 stick) unsalted butter
Herbs for seasoning: salt,
  pepper, sage, thyme, garlic
16 cups of 1-inch salt rising
  bread cubes (1½# loaf)

PREPARATION

1. Melt the butter.
2. Mince herbs and/or garlic;
   mix with the melted butter
   to steam.
3. Pour seasoned butter evenly
   over the bread cubes.
4. Cool croutons before placing
   in a bag.
5. Use the croutons in salads
   or soups.

Taming the Wild Microbes: Salt Rising Bread Starters

Featuring Barb Morris, Mt. Morris, Pennsylvania

Letha Fink, Fairview, West Virginia

Joyce Varner, Durbin West Virginia

The mysteries abound when it comes to understanding salt rising bread. One certainty that bakers of authentic salt rising bread must understand and strictly adhere to is that traditional salt rising bread does not ever use added yeast for purposes of making the bread rise. Not only does adding yeast overpower the wonderful cheese-like flavor and smell of the bread, a successful starter simply does not need the yeast to raise the dough. Instead, the rising power comes from the wild microbes in the grains and starches of the starter ingredients – flour, cornmeal, and/or potato.

The Starter

The first step in baking salt rising bread is to make a starter (sometimes called *risin'* or *raisin'*). There are hundreds of different recipes for starters, which sometimes vary slightly and sometimes a lot. Salt rising bread recipes from the early 1800s include strange instructions such as "scald the earthen vessel" or "scald the Indian meal" or "make a Railroad yeast" (see glossary and page 52). However, we have found that there are really two basic salt rising bread recipes. Over the years, we have spent considerable time researching, testing and perfecting these two recipes. Our first recipe uses potatoes, flour and sugar, baking soda and boiling water. The second recipe uses cornmeal, flour, baking soda and heated milk.

1. SALT RISING BREAD STARTER WITH POTATOES

INGREDIENTS

3-4 medium size potatoes
2 T sugar
1 heaping tsp. baking soda

Boiling water, enough to cover potatoes
3 T flour

PREPARATION

1. Slice potatoes, with the peel on or off, into a bowl or jar.
2. Add the sugar and baking soda.
3. Pour boiling water over this mixture to cover the potatoes.
4. Sprinkle the flour over the potatoes.
5. Cover the container with a cloth and keep in a warm place overnight, until bubbly and foamy.

2. SALT RISING BREAD STARTER WITH CORNMEAL AND MILK

INGREDIENTS

3 T cornmeal

1 T all-purpose flour

½ heaping tsp. baking soda

½ cup scalded milk (170°F) (77°C)

PREPARATION

1. Combine the cornmeal, flour, and baking soda in a small bowl or jar.
2. Pour the heated milk over this mixture and stir.
3. Cover the container with a cloth and keep in a warm place overnight, until bubbly and foamy.

Note: The starter benefits from the addition of baking soda, as it is thought that such buffering agents can suppress the growth of yeast and thereby enable the less competitive bacteria to reproduce. It's also possible that baking soda enhances bacteria more than it suppresses yeast. Another area for a microbiologist to investigate!

For each of these recipes, the starter is put in a warm place to ferment at the correct temperature overnight. After 9 to 12 hours the starter should be ready. This is a crucial point in the success of salt rising bread. If the starter doesn't ferment enough, then the sponge and dough stage won't rise. If the starter is allowed to ferment too long, then a similar failed attempt will result. The precise fermentation time varies with ingredients and conditions (this is where wild microbes differ from commercial yeast).

Time and Temperature

Time and temperature are two critical variables. It doesn't matter what time you begin your starter, as long as you are present near the end of the fermentation time in order to catch the starter at its peak. A baker can begin the starter the previous evening to make sponge and bread during the following day. Or, making a starter in the morning can work just as well for a baker who wants to complete the bread during the evening hours. If you miss the time that the starter is ready to be made into a sponge, your sponge will not rise and, thus, neither will your bread. Use caution when experimenting with salt rising bread because the starter has its own mysterious rhythm, usually unbeknownst to the baker, and the fermentation in the starter will be ready according to its own complex set of rules and conditions.

Home-size digital water bath

A good baker who is familiar with the variances of a starter can utilize the knowledge of timing to his or her advantage. For instance, at the bakery, we set our starters of an evening to be ready at specific times early the next morning, so the baker knows when to show up for work.

The heat source for the salt rising starter is critical. It must be consistent and be able to hover, ideally, around 105°F (40.5°C). The temperature can go a bit lower or even as high as 113°F (45°C) without guaranteed failure. But these temperature changes will alter the timing and final readiness of the starter.

When Timing is Everything

An 80-year-old gentleman wrote to Susan's Salt Rising Bread Project website with his story of unfortunate timing:

> One Friday night I mixed up a batch of ingredients and Saturday morning the
> starter had begun to work. I added some flour, and the next step usually requires
> several hours. I had promised my wife that I would take her shopping, so I put
> the starter on top of the refrigerator to keep warm, and we went to New Jersey
> shopping. The trip took longer than I anticipated and, when we returned, there
> was a mess awaiting us, or should I say me. The batter had risen to the top of
> the bowl, overflowed, and dripped down the back of the refrigerator all over the
> cooling coils. These coils are warm and the goop had dried. It was quite a chore
> to clean up!

How to tell when a starter is ready. The baker must learn to identify when a starter is ready by observing the foam that forms on the surface of the starter liquid, as well as a particular fermented odor. Thus, the first good indicator of readiness is when the foam is at its highest peak or when it ceases to increase in volume. The second good indicator of readiness is when the *slight* inhalation of air at the mouth of the starter jar causes one's face to scrunch up with distaste. Yes, this is when the odor is the most unpleasant! Careful observations conducted towards the end of the fermentation period are necessary at first, to identify when fermentation has reached its height. With experience, the baker will become skilled in identifying when a starter is ready. Then, the sponge stage can be completed, and the rest of the bread making procedure is the same with either starter.

Jar of foamy starter

So, here we have two quite different recipes that vary in their ingredients and preparation – yet how is it possible that we end up with bread that cannot be distinguished one from the other? [*Jenny's note:* Okay, maybe Susan can tell which bread was made from which starter, but she's one of the world's experts on salt rising bread! We challenge anyone to determine which bread came from which starter.]

Does it really matter what's in your starter?

Reinald Nielsen, a fellow devoté of salt rising bread whom we met via the Internet, carried out many interesting experiments using various grains in starter recipes other than potatoes or cornmeal. He used oat bran, steel cut oats, wheat bran, wheat germ, wheat gluten, wheat flakes, spelt flakes, triticale, shredded wheat biscuits, barley, white and yellow cornmeal, processed cornmeal, kamut flour, buckwheat flour, white and whole wheat flour. All of these made successful starters. He also used tree bark, specifically white oak and black locust, and found that these barks made excellent initiators for salt rising bread starters as well. "Common cheese and blue cheese also initiate distinctive starters," he said. Curiously, the bread tastes much the same no matter the starter used.

Another ingredient that Reinald claimed increased the success rate of his starters was a quarter of a Campden tablet (traditionally used to make beer and wine). [*Susan's observation:* I once tried adding a partial Campden tablet to my starter and woke up early the next morning thinking my septic tank had overflowed. I barely got downstairs before I realized the smell was the salt rising bread starter ready to go! But the smell was too strong, and I tossed the starter over the hill immediately.]

Other Starters: Railroad Yeast

There are some recipes that don't use any cornmeal or potatoes – the only grain is flour – and other recipes that include ginger. We have a few recipes with ginger in the starter (one very old recipe said that the purpose of ginger was to keep the starter warm). And then there was something called railroad yeast (see glossary); its unusual name has yet to be explained in the sources we have consulted, and there appear to be variations.

Here is an 1882 recipe for making railroad yeast, from Susan's collection – from *The California Practical Cook Book*: One half pint middlings, one half teaspoonful each of salt, ginger, soda and sugar. Mix all together and scald with one half pint of boiling water; let it rise for twelve hours, keep warm until light.

Salt rising bread, using railroad yeast. We found this 1896 recipe in *Baxter's Practical Up-To-Date Receipt Book for Bakers,* by Richard Baxter, written for professional bakers and dedicated "To the Bakers of America."

Salt Rising Bread

This is perhaps the most difficult bread to make, but it is a good seller if it is made right. The following formula is about the best one I ever tried and it is a good one.

Set a Railroad [sic] yeast with equal parts of ginger, sugar, salt and soda, about 1 teaspoonful altogether, in a quart bowl. Pour 1 pt. boiling water in the bowl and stir well, adding enough canell, or middlings, to make stiff batter.

Keep this in a warm place about 7 hours, when it will be light. Set sponge with this, using about 2½ qts. of lukewarm water, and keep in a warm place to rise again. When this sponge is light, add 2½ qts. more of lukewarm water, and 4 oz. salt. Then mix and scale off and put into pans. When light, bake.

Always keep this bread in a warm place, as it needs much "nursing." If it gets chilled, the batch is lost.

Use all winter wheat flour.

About Commercial Yeast

Commercial yeast, the scientific name being *Saccharomyces cerevisiae*, was first made available in the 1860s. Before then, women who made yeasted breads often found their own wild yeast by skimming off the "barm" from beer-making. Because the barm was comprised of wild yeasts and bacteria, the timing of rising/baking bread from barm yeast was unpredictable, similar to salt rising bread. In current times, *S. cerevisiae* has been extensively researched and its genetics are valuable tools in molecular and cell biology. Because yeast DNA has more similarities to human DNA than bacterial DNA, many of the proteins that yeasts produce have led to important discoveries in the medical field that have improved our health. *S. cerevisiae* for baking is now a very stable and predictable ingredient when used to raise bread.

Reasons why salt rising bread starters can fail:

- Starter can be left too long and bacteria run out of food and begin to die
- Starter can be used too soon, and doesn't have enough of the required bacteria to raise the sponge
- Temperature of the starter is not set correctly or is not consistent; ideal is 104°-110°F (40-43°C)
- Potatoes have green on them
- Potatoes, cornmeal, or flour is too old
- Plastic wrap covering jar should not be airtight; you don't want a vacuum forming inside the jar.
- Starters made in plastic containers tend to fail more often. Glass, metal or ceramic containers are recommended.

Our search for more history and lore about salt rising bread starters continues:

Barb Morris

We went to visit Barb Morris in the summertime. She lives just down the road from Susan in our lovely, Appalachian town of Mt. Morris, Pennsylvania. Barb is married to Wes Morris whose great, great, great grandfather originally settled this sleepy little town. We describe Mt. Morris as sleepy because it used to be a booming oil town at the turn of the 20th century. The oil boom came and went, just as coal mining in the area is currently doing. But the town is beginning to wake up again due to urban sprawl crawling north from Morgantown, West Virginia, and because there is intense fracking in the rural back hills, with drill bits going two miles down.

Barb's grandmother was famous in this area for her salt rising bread, and Barb is excited to tell us about how she learned to make it. She begins her salt rising bread history with a description of her grandmother, Mae Johnson.

Barb Morris

Mae Johnson was born in 1884 and died in 1974, at the age of 90. She was brought up on salt rising bread, and she made it herself. Mae was only 4 feet 8 inches tall and was in her early teens when her mother left the family with another man. Since Mae was the oldest, her father got her a stool so that she could now make the bread for her family. Mae's mother never came back.

After a while, the conversation turned to the starter that Barb uses. We were eager to know her recipe and particular technique.

Sometimes it comes and sometimes it doesn't. My grandmother's recipe uses 3 medium-sized potatoes, ¼ teaspoon of soda and ¼ teaspoon of salt. Then you pour 4 cups of boiling water over top of that. On top of the jar of boiled water

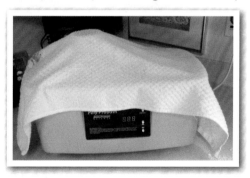

and potatoes, you sprinkle 3 tablespoons of flour (it is not necessary to stir in the flour), then cover the jar with a lid. Take your crockpot and put a plate on top, then a large, heavy pie plate, then a smaller pie plate, then the bowl of starter. Then cover the bowl with a tea towel. Put the crockpot on low. The heat from my crockpot stays steady, and this is what you want. I set it around 3 to 4 o'clock in the afternoon. When I get up in the morning and it has suds on top, it's ready, usually about 5:30 a.m. And, it smells! When my friends come get me for an early walk, they say, "Oh, Barb! You must have a sewer backed up." But the smell doesn't bother me at all.

[Jenny] What intrigued us about Barb's recipe was the lack of cornmeal in it and the long time it takes her starter to ferment. At the bakery, our original potato starter recipe included cornmeal. The starter usually fermented in 8 to 10 hours. We found that when we omit the cornmeal, the starter will take 1 to 2 hours longer to work.

This past year, we struggled to find a reliable cornmeal. For a while, we tried field corn from Jackson's Mill, West Virginia, that was freshly ground just before we purchased it. Later, we bought field corn from a local farmer and ground it ourselves. This made a starter that would be ready in 9 hours or less! But, the farmer's corn eventually went to feed his cows by the end of March, so we had to find a new source. Since Susan's grandmother always used store-bought cornmeal successfully in her starters, we tried cornmeal from Krogers, and it worked well, with the starters taking an hour or two longer to ferment than the freshly-ground field corn had. It was after our visit with Barb Morris that we had an aha! moment. We don't need to put cornmeal in our starter! Now, we regularly leave cornmeal out of our starters at the bakery.

The Salt in Salt Rising Bread

Over the years, we have learned so much from the bread-baking elders of this region of Appalachia, who have helped us unlock the mysteries of our favorite bread. This one has to do with salt – the type of salt you use in your starter.

One ingredient that is often common in salt rising bread starters is some type of salt. The salt can be common table salt (NaCl) or it can be a type of chemical salt, such as baking soda or saleratus (see glossary and page 40). Please note in our potato recipe (page 48) that baking soda is used. In Chapter 3, we told why we switched from table salt to baking soda for our starters at the bakery, in order to increase the "salt rising bread smell."

Some Frank Advice from Two Baking Elders

Letha Fink

Letha Fink

Letha Fink learned how to make her salt rising bread from Ora Gump, who was her neighbor from nearby Fairview, West Virginia. We consider Fairview to be one of the capitals of salt rising bread, because almost everyone in Fairview has either a relative or an elderly neighbor who used to make it. Fairview also exemplifies the rural beauty of many of the small towns in this mountain state. The road leading into Fairview heads down from steep hills on all sides into a large bowl. All the roads in West Virginia follow a stream or creek, and this one is no different. The road bends and curves right along the stream bed, with the dark, green rhododendrons hovering under a canopy of large oaks and maples. This makes for a cool, shaded ride in the heat of summer, with dappled light playing through the leaves as we swerve up and around one last hill crest before entering the center of town.

Fairview is isolated enough from other small towns that the community of people who settled here shared their lives similarly to how people still do in rural villages all over the world. A warm, supportive culture still thrives! The Fairview Diner feeds locals with good, homemade fare and is the place to go when you need to find out some information. Of course, there is a Dollar Store and across the street there is a large, empty storefront with antique glass cases for some ambitious retailer.

Although we have yet to hear of anyone who has died from either eating or making salt rising bread, this sentiment from Letha is certainly common among bakers of this bread: "Salt rising bread will kill you with work! It's hard, and it's a lost art."

Letha repeats these words that every successful salt rising baker knows:

You can't be in a hurry when making salt rising bread, you must have patience. It has its own mind and will take as long as it needs, regardless of the baker's input. When I see that it has worked, I jump up and down! It can drive you nuts. That's for sure!

3 Ways to Give Salt Rising Bread a Boost, Resulting in a Shorter Fermentation Time:

1. **Freezing:** after your sponge (second stage) has risen, remove 1 cup of the batter and put it in a closed container or a plastic bag and place it in your freezer. When you are ready to set a new starter, remove the frozen sponge from the freezer and allow it to thaw at room temperature. Then, add it to the starter recipe and set to ferment as usual. It should be ready in 4 to 5 hours.

2. **Drying:** after your sponge (second stage) has risen, remove HALF a cup of the batter and spread it on a large plate with a spoon. Allow this to dry at room temperature for about 24 hours, until it is very dry and it cracks. When it is dry, crumble it up and place it in an airtight container. When you are ready to set a new starter, add the crumbles to the starter recipe and mix in well. Set the starter to ferment as usual. It should be ready in 4 to 5 hours.

3. **Saving a wad of dough:** Save about a half-pound of salt rising bread dough after it has been worked. Bury this in a bowl of flour or keep in the refrigerator. The next morning, stir the dough in a bowl with a quart of warm water to soften the dough. Add flour to make a thick batter (similar to a sponge). Set it to rise until double in bulk. Proceed with the recipe to make dough as usual.

Joyce Varner

A few months later, we were in Durbin, West Virginia, on a visit with Joyce Varner. It was a warm autumn afternoon, with the fall foliage in full color as we traveled over the back country roads. Joyce is another avid salt rising bread baker who readily tells us many stories of making salt rising bread over the past 40 years. We sit quietly and comfortably on her pleasant side porch, with a mountain breeze to cool us, as she entertains us with stories of her neighbor who taught her how to make this bread. With a grin, Joyce says:

Did you ever have a failure? My neighbor, Old Lady Keller, said to me that salt rising bread is just like a typical virgin – you never know what it's going to do. I don't care how many times you make it, it will be different each time. Sometimes, it's beautiful and, when you slice it, it is just like pound cake. Then, you'll make it three or four times, and it won't come up at all. Sometimes, you just have to pray for it to rise. When it doesn't work, I put it back in the flour sack and ask someone to haul it away.

Joyce Varner and Susan

Joyce was eager to tell us that Old Lady Keller had taught her how to extend a sponge by saving a wad of the salt rising dough. A sponge made this way will take nearly half the time to double that it takes a typical salt rising bread sponge to double.

[Jenny] We've tried this method in the bakery with great success, and it has enabled us to get an additional batch of bread out in the same day. Joyce also suggests that a salt rising bread starter can be successfully made using potato flakes instead of potatoes, although we have never tried doing that.

Joyce worked in the local schools and was able to procure one of the 20-quart Hobart mixers the school was giving away. How lucky she was, because the mixer enabled her to make 15 to 20 loaves at a time, at home, with no hand kneading. People in that small community wanted salt rising bread, and she was able to fulfill the demand!

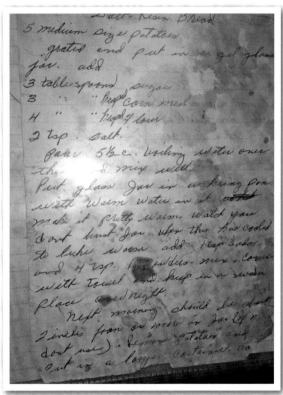

Joyce Varner's well-used recipe

Folklore Develops to Explain a Temperamental Bread

In his 1904 memoir of life in early Illinois, *Juliet and Joliet*, William Grinton writes:

Those were the days of salt rising bread, saleratus biscuits, and dried apple pies. The salt rising bread required not only skill but luck. It could be brought out of the oven in perfection only when the moon was in the right quarter and the wind was not in the east. While it was rising, boys had to tread softly, whistle in a low key and not slam the doors. The cat and dog were shut out, and the girls were not allowed to giggle in the kitchen. The bread makers always spoke of having good luck or bad luck with their baking, and the temper of the lady was usually in harmony with the bread.

William Grinton couldn't have described this scene of a salt rising bread baking day more accurately! His use of the word harmony is particularly fitting. After many years of making salt rising bread, I [Susan] have come to understand that being in harmony with the bread as you prepare and then await the conclusion of each stage is critical to the success of this endeavor. I like to call it SRBeing, meaning being at one with salt rising bread and all its stages. This may sound crazy to some, but I sincerely believe in it.

I can almost always predict when my bread will fail. It happens when I am not paying enough attention to the "demands" of the starter, the sponge, or the dough. It feels to me like it's about respecting the process and the life that this process is creating. I like to think of it as being like little children who "get it" when they are in loving and capable hands. SRBeing allows the bread baker to "get it."

A lot of wonderful folklore surrounds the making of salt rising bread, and stories of failures are quite familiar with everyone who has ever attempted to make it. Some people blame the failure on the weather: it was too cool or too humid, or rain was just about to set in. Others believe their failure was due to having used new potatoes rather than old, or having used the wrong kind of cornmeal in the starter. Some have even attributed their failure to the "time of the month" of the woman doing the baking. Because salt rising bread starters capture wild bacteria, failures occur for different reasons, but salt rising bread bakers have always blamed them on any number of variables that happen to be occurring at the time.

Our dear friend Pearl Haines knew this all too well:

> *When I was pregnant, I couldn't get the starter to come, so my husband would make it. And, sometimes, it seemed like it failed due to the weather. But weather makes a good thing to blame it on. You must have patience to make salt raisin' bread successfully. You must pay attention, and you cannot hurry it along. I would make my starter early of an evening, whereupon it would be ready early the next morning. Then, I'd add flour to make my sponge and let that raise up. For many, many years I made five loaves on Tuesday and twelve loaves on Friday. As for failures, I didn't have many, maybe two or three over a 90-year period. The only failures I had were the starters not coming.*

Pearl had mastered what it took to be a successful salt rising bread baker – always reminding us of the most important thing:

> **"YOU MUST PAY ATTENTION, AND YOU CANNOT HURRY IT ALONG."**

PIZZA WITH SALT RISING BREAD CRUST

INGREDIENTS

Salt rising bread dough
Pizza sauce and toppings

PREPARATION

1. Follow your favorite salt rising bread recipe to make a soft dough.
2. On a floured surface, roll out enough dough (about 2 pounds) to fill a lightly greased pizza pan.
3. Fill pan with pizza dough and add desired sauce and toppings.
4. Bake at 500° F (260° C) for 15 to 20 minutes, until crust is golden.

⊙ SALT RISING BREAD ROLLS ⊛

INGREDIENTS

Salt rising bread dough
Butter, apple butter, jam,
    gravy, or other desired
    accompaniments for rolls

PREPARATION

1. Follow your favorite salt rising bread recipe to make a soft dough.

2. On a floured surface, pinch off dough pieces (3 oz. each) to smaller than a tennis ball, larger than a ping-pong ball.

3. Roll each dough piece into a smooth ball, bringing all the edges together on the under side. Pinch edges together.

4. Place rolls touching each other on a lightly greased cookie sheet or pie pan.

5. Let rolls rise until almost double, then bake at 375° F (190.5° C) for 10 to 12 minutes.

6. Put rolls under the broiler for 2 to 3 minutes for a golden finish.

7. Serve with butter, jam, apple butter, or gravy.

SIX

The Perfect Loaf: 12 Secrets to Success

Featuring Alma Davis of Bridgeport, West Virginia

☙❧

Sitting in a small but cozy living room, with handmade quilts on the couch and the familiar smell of salt rising bread coming from the country kitchen, we feel as if we are in the home of a longtime friend. We have, however, only just met Alma Davis. Very soon, we begin to learn just what a special person she is.

> *I'm a pioneer lady. You name it, I've done it. I went to a one-room schoolhouse*
> *for first through third grade. I've had vision in only my left eye and hearing in*
> *only my left ear since I was four years old. I've sewn many quilts in my lifetime.*
> *I've had breast cancer, but I don't drink coffee, and I have never smoked. I've*
> *been alone for 25 years, since my husband died. But I'm not depressed. I teach*
> *Sunday school, and I still drive. Plus, I cut my own grass.*

Alma lives just outside of Bridgeport, West Virginia. We have come on a sunny spring day in April to talk with her about salt rising bread.

I'm not for fancy cakes, and I don't eat very many sweets. But because I love a challenge, I began making salt rising bread 12 years ago, at the age of 76. I had made regular bread for my family for years. My mother loved salt rising bread and wanted some. With an old cookbook in hand, I was able to bake some for my dear mother. The recipe I used didn't give much direction, as the secret is in what you do.

Alma Davis

As we listened to Alma describe the steps and strategies of her technique, we knew we were also hearing the voices of many a pioneer woman who had come before, learning from trial and error to make a perfect loaf of salt rising bread. Here, then, is what Alma told us, which aligns with what we have learned about success with salt rising bread:

SECRET #1: Keep the starter warm, at about 104-110°F (40-43°C). Every thermometer is different, hence keeping your starter at these approximate temperatures will ensure a proper fermentation.

I use a three-step method. I tried lots of different ways for my starter and finally got success with using my canner. I put water in the canner and set it on a hot plate. Then I put another pot inside the canner with water in it and bring it up to temperature with a thermometer before I begin my starter. The thermometer needs to read 110°F (43°C).

SECRET #2: Place some baking soda in your starter to help with the fermentation. This can make for a smellier bread, which is a good thing!

About 4:00 p.m., I take 2 medium pota- toes, peel them and put them in a jar. Then, place 2 tablespoons sugar, 2 tablespoons flour, 2 tablespoons cornmeal (I always use yellow cornmeal) and, finally, ¼ teaspoon baking soda on top of the potatoes. Get your water almost boiling, and pour it over all these ingredients. Cover the jar with aluminum foil and poke a slit in it for air to get in. Place the jar in the inside pot that has water in it, which is inside the warmed canner, which also has water in it.

SECRET #3: Make more than one starter, in case one of them doesn't work. We do this at the bakery all the time. Remember, since you are working with wild microbes, the chances of one starter not working are high! Starters can take from 9 to 14 hours to be ready. If there is no foam after 8 or more hours, simply shake the starter to speed things up.

Usually, I'll prepare at least 2 and sometimes 3 jars of starter. During this time, I keep close watch on the thermometer so that it stays at 110°F (43°C). Then, I'll go to bed. If it has worked, I can smell it in the morning. It smells real bad, but that's a good sign!

SECRET #4: Keep your sponge warm, again at around 104-110°F (40-43°C). Check the warmth often because it could get too hot or it could cool down too much.

To make my sponge, I take one jar out, and empty all the ingredients and potato slices into a bowl that has already been warmed. Gingerly, I pick up each potato slice, squish it with my fingers, and wash it clean in the same bowl. Next, I discard the potatoes if I only want to make a few loaves. If I want to make 20 or more loaves, I'll tell you what else I do after (see page 74). But for now, into this liquid, I add enough flour to make a pancake-like batter and then set this bowl in a pan of warm water on top of a hot pad. If the bowl gets cold, I put a little heat under the pan to keep the sponge warm. This will rise up until it gets to the top of the bowl. This can take a long time, but sometimes it is faster than other times. Patience is what you need!

SECRET #5: Many types of cornmeal can be successfully used in salt rising bread. Opinions vary on which one works the best, but we have found that freshly ground cornmeal, store-bought cornmeal, and both white and yellow cornmeal all have the potential to work equally well. The real culprit in the failure of a starter is not just the cornmeal, but the many conditions that need to all come together to make it work.

SECRET #6: Never use the green part on a potato. At the bakery and at home, we have found the green spots can inhibit the wild microbes from raising the starter.

SECRET #7: Be patient! You have already waited overnight for the starter to work; a couple more hours and you'll have bread! Each sponge is unique so the doubling time is often different on different days. On average, the sponge should double in 1 to 2 hours. If the sponge takes longer than 4 hours, we recommend throwing it out instead of wasting your time and flour to make dough.

Fermented sponge

SECRET #8: Keep the dough warm. The proofer at the bakery warms our dough perfectly. Home bakers can use their ovens set at 100°F (38°C) to proof their bread.

When the sponge is ready to make into dough, I combine 2 cups of hot water, an egg-size scoop of Crisco, 2 tablespoons of sugar, and 1½ teaspoons of salt. Next, I add some flour before I put the sponge in, and I mix it well. Then I add the sponge while the bowl and ingredients are hot. This heat is so important for salt rising bread. I can't emphasize it enough. My friend said that she would put a half package of yeast in her dough, but that is cheating. I divide my dough and weigh each portion. I use my mother's pans, and each loaf weighs around 2¼ pounds. Shortening is spread on top of each loaf, before and after it is baked. The dough rises in a warm oven, which I keep warm by first turning the oven on for a few minutes. Then I turn off the oven and turn on the oven light. For additional heat, I even put in a 100-watt light bulb on the end of an extension cord and place it on the bottom shelf, with the loaves on the top shelf of the oven.

SECRET #9: Place the proper amount of dough in the pan. A good rule is to place 1½ pounds of dough in an average bread pan. Please note that some bread pans are larger or smaller than others.

SECRET #10: Allow your dough to rise up to the top edge of the bread pan. If you don't do this, you often see a horizontal crack alongside the finished loaf, just below the upper crust. This cracking happens because the heat gets to the outer layers of dough before the inner layers. If the inner layers haven't risen to their potential, they will continue to push up the outer layers and form the crack. This can also happen if you have too much dough in your pan (see Secret #9).

When the loaves have risen, I remove the loaves in order to preheat the oven for the baking. The bread is baked at 350°F (175°C) for 45 minutes.

SECRET #11: You can increase your yield well beyond 2 or 3 loaves by utilizing Alma's tip on the next page, without having to wait overnight for another round of starters to work. More tricks for jumpstarting a new batch of loaves can be found on page 59.

Alma's Tip for Making 20 Loaves or More

Now, if I want to make 20 loaves or more, I can use two methods. First, I use the other 2 jars of starter. Follow instructions as before to make a sponge from each starter. Once the sponge rises, make your dough. For the 2nd method, you can reuse the potato slices to make a second round of starter. Place these washed potato slices back in a jar, add the same starter ingredients as before, and set the jars in the pot that is inside the canner. It's real important to keep checking the temperature of the water in the pot to make sure it stays around 110°F (43°C). The second round of starter only takes 2 to 3 hours to be ready to make into a sponge.

We sit back and take in every word that Alma so earnestly shares with us. "I never baked this beloved bread for income," she says, as our visit draws to a close. "I can't make salt rising bread anymore because I am 88 years old and can't stand long enough to knead it."

We said there would be 12 secrets in this chapter, so what is Secret #12? It's Alma's parting advice:

"Just live!"

◑

An Easier, Quicker Way to Make a Perfect Loaf

[Susan] I have good news for the baker who may not always have the time to devote to a classic recipe for salt rising bread. It's possible to make an excellent loaf by skipping the one-to-two hour sponge/batter stage. Fortunately, there are a few recipes that show us how. The recipe below is one of those. It skips the sponge/batter stage by making up the dough directly from the successful starter. This is desirable for two reasons. First, it shortens the amount of time it takes to finish the bread, and second, it relieves the baker's worry about whether or not the sponge is working and whether it is ready to be made into the dough.

This recipe was originally printed in 1935 in *The Household Searchlight Recipe Book.* My paternal grandmother's sister, Gladys Huff Burr, made this recipe for many years for her family and friends. It was passed on to me by Gladys' niece, Alice Brown Juergens, who is my beloved Aunt Pinky.

∾ NO-SPONGE SALT RISING BREAD RECIPE ∾

YIELD: 3 LOAVES

STARTER

3 medium potatoes
3 T cornmeal
1 tsp. sugar

1 tsp. salt
4 cups boiling water

DOUGH

2 cups lukewarm milk
1 cup water
1/8 tsp. baking soda
1/8 tsp. salt

2 T melted shortening
Flour enough to make a stiff dough,
   about 3-4 cups

PREPARATION

1. Slice and pare the potatoes. Add cornmeal, sugar, salt and water. Wrap in a heavy cloth and allow to stand in a warm place overnight.
2. In the morning, remove potatoes. Add milk, water, soda, salt and shortening.
3. Add enough flour to make a stiff dough for kneading. Knead until smooth.
4. Place in 3 greased bread pans and allow to rise until double in size.
5. Bake at 400°F (210°C) for 30-45 minutes, until golden brown.

☙ ALMA DAVIS'S SALT RISING BREAD RECIPE ❧

STARTER

1. About 4:00 in the afternoon, peel 2 medium potatoes and put them in a jar.
2. Add 2 T each of sugar, flour and cornmeal (I always use yellow cornmeal).
3. Add ¼ tsp. baking soda on top of everything.
4. Pour almost boiling water over all these ingredients.
5. Keep a close watch on the thermometer and keep constant warmth at 110°F (43°C) overnight.

SPONGE

1. The next morning, after the starter is foamy and bubbly, warm a bowl and empty all the ingredients into it.
2. Gingerly, pick up each potato slice and wash it clean in the same bowl. Set potato slices aside for later use, if desired.
3. Into this liquid, add enough flour to make a pancake-like batter.
4. Set bowl in a pan of warm water, on top of a hot pad. If bowl gets cold, put a little heat under the pan to keep the sponge warm.
5. Let sponge rise to the top of the bowl. It can take a long time, but sometimes it is faster than other times. Patience is what you need!

DOUGH

When the sponge has doubled in size, it is ready to make into dough.

1. Combine in a bowl 2 cups hot water, an egg-size scoop of Crisco, 2 T sugar, and 1½ tsp. salt.
2. Add the sponge and enough flour to make a soft dough. Mix it well. Keep the bowl and ingredients hot. This heat is critical for the success of salt rising bread.

3. Divide the dough and weigh each portion to approximately 2¼ pounds (the amount of dough will vary depending on the size of your bread pans). Spread shortening on top of each loaf before and after it is baked.

4. Turn on the oven for a few minutes to get warm. Then, turn off the oven but keep the oven light on. For additional heat, you can put a 100-watt light bulb on the end of an extension cord and place it on the bottom shelf with the loaves on the top shelf of the oven.

5. When the loaves have risen, remove the loaves and preheat the oven to 350°F (175°C).

6. Bake for 45 minutes.

Tomato Sandwich Time!

People dream all winter about the luscious tomatoes of summer. It's hard to come by a better summertime sandwich than this one, especially one made with salt rising bread!

๑ GARDEN TOMATO SANDWICH ๏

INGREDIENTS

2 slices salt rising bread
2 T butter or mayonnaise
2 slices cucumber

4 slices fresh garden tomato
Salt and pepper to taste

PREPARATION

1. Using fresh, thinly sliced salt rising bread, spread butter or mayonnaise on two slices of bread.

2. Add the tomato slices and cucumber slices.

3. Add salt and pepper to taste.

Bread may be toasted, if preferred.

FRIED GREEN TOMATO SANDWICH

INGREDIENTS

1 green tomato
3 T flour
2 T vegetable oil

2 slices salt rising bread
2 T butter or mayonnaise
Salt and pepper to taste

PREPARATION

1. Slice the tomato and coat slices with flour.

2. Fry the tomato slices in hot oil until brown on both sides.

3. Using fresh, thinly sliced salt rising bread, spread butter or mayonnaise on two slices of bread.

4. Add the fried green tomato slices.

5. Add salt and pepper to taste.

Bread may be toasted, if preferred.

Almost as Good as Grandma's: Commercial Bakeries and Salt Rising Bread

Featuring Jack Ward of Nicholasville, Kentucky

Bill Crum of Olatle, Kansas

Van de Kamp's bakeries on the West Coast

As the burgeoning cities of Colonial America expanded and thrived, commercial bakeries became established, supplying bread to homes that didn't have ovens and to local pubs. Typically, these bakeries, such as in Boston and Philadelphia, were crude-looking buildings with high open windows to let the heat out and the light in. Stepping inside, you would see troughs that held large batches of sponges and doughs at different stages of bread making. Alongside would be buckets of water, bags of flour, and salt. The baker worked long, hard hours from dawn to dusk kneading doughs by hand and baking bread in wood-fired ovens.

Meanwhile, in the more isolated rural areas the pioneer housewife proudly practiced her baking skills, passing them down to her daughters and granddaughters as they had been passed down to her – as part of the daily routine of life at that time. There was no reason to write down what worked, unless perhaps in a diary, so the knowledge became part of an oral history tradition. Traditional baking skills and recipes were practiced and honored across the land.

When we jump forward in time to the 1920s, we see towns and cities everywhere, with running water and electricity – and 80-quart Hobart mixers had been invented! These

machines could knead large batches of dough, which led commercial bakeries to their heyday. There is no evidence of any commercial bakery selling salt rising bread before commercial mixers were available. So, with the advent of Hobart's wonderful invention, bake it they did!

Jenny knows from first-hand the joys and challenges of baking salt rising bread commercially. But what must it have been like for a baker 50 or more years ago? And how did their process, and their bread, differ from the traditional ways of the home baker? We were privileged to interview two "elder" commercial bakers to hear their stories.

Baker Jack Ward

When we met Jack he was approaching 90, and his wife wasn't far behind. For many years, Jack and his wife owned a commercial bakery in Nicholasville, Kentucky, and baked salt rising bread there. Several customers from Rising Creek had mentioned Jack's bakery, just outside of Lexington, which is how we found out about it. Jack and Madeline Ward were glad to talk to us and invited us to come visit. It was a day's drive through the hills of southern West Virginia, west over the gentler hills of Kentucky, past Berea College, and on the other side of Lexington. Here is Jack's story, as he told it to us:

Jack Ward

My dad started a bakery in 1927. He did his baking out of the old coke ovens that stayed hot all day. Soon, World War II came, and all the men left for war. That is when my brothers and I began working in the bakery. I was 15 years old, and it was 1942. We quit school and never left the bakery. All of my relatives were either bakers or started their own bakeries throughout the coming years.

There was a demand for salt rising bread, but my dad didn't know how to make it. He was taught how to make this bread from an elderly African-American man who came down from Lexington to teach him the recipe. This salt rising bread recipe was a cornmeal-milk starter with lard brushed on top. My dad passed the recipe on to me. But, as always, there were recurring failures when making it.

Luckily for Jack's dad, there was help available for salt rising bread failures. In Chapter 3, we described Governor Stubbs' 1909 campaign to provide housewives with a no-fail type of yeast for their salt rising bread, and how Stubbs funded a young scientist, Dr. Henry Kohman, to do this. He developed and patented Kohman's Salt Rising Yeast in the early 'teens and sold it to commercial bakeries for many years. King Arthur Flour Company later sold the product to home bakers until the mid-1990s. By the 1950s, virtually all the commercial bakeries that produced salt rising bread in the United States purchased Kohman's yeast and were baking (mostly) successful batches of salt rising bread. Strangely, though, while commercial bakeries were enthusiastically using Kohman's yeast, home bakers apparently were not using it (contrary to Governor Stubbs' original intent). Perhaps there wasn't enough profit in the home market to package small amounts of Kohman's yeast for home bakers – until King Arthur Flour Company. We have only ever seen bulk bags for Kohman's yeast sold to bakeries.

Jack continues:

> When Kohman's yeast became available, my dad started using it, and he swore by it. I would begin the salt rising bread starter with Kohman's yeast in the early evening, around 8:00 p.m. Then, I'd get to the bakery at 3:00 a.m., and check the starter at 5:00 a.m., about nine hours later. For my cornmeal-milk starter, I used high heat powdered milk, since I was adding scalding water to it. My starter would be thick and mushy. When it got real smelly, then it was ready. For the sponge, I'd add water and milk. Did I tell you we still had failures? Oh yeah!

> Because the demand was high, my dad would make 200 loaf batches on a Saturday. To avoid further failures, my dad also used Kohman's Improver, which was added to the sponge, especially if it seemed that the sponge was going to run out of rising power.

By 1918 Kohman had a second patent, called Kohman's Improver, a powder that contained calcium carbonate and potassium iodate, chemicals that seemed to stabilize the sponge stage, enabling it to rise with more uniformity.

Once salt rising bread could be baked more reliably, commercial bakeries began producing loaves, because they no longer had to be concerned about lost revenues from failures. While Kohman's yeast did give bakers a higher rate of success with their salt rising bread, failures and losses continued to plague home bakers and bakeries. Consequently, bakeries increasingly began to add bread baker's yeast *(Saccharomyces cerevisiae)* to the bread, along with Kohman's yeast. Although traditional salt rising bread recipes never incorporate baker's yeast, the adoption of *S. cerevisiae* in salt rising bread recipes became common practice in bakeries, making failures with salt rising bread far less frequent.

Kohman's instructions for making salt rising bread yeast can be found in scientific journals, and his patent is available for viewing. We were able to formulate a similar yeast at our bakery, but found we didn't need it to reliably produce salt rising bread. We continue to do it the old-fashioned way.

Kohman's patented instructions were sold several times throughout the 20th century, first to Roland Industries in 1939, and then to Plantation Pride in Virginia in 1965. Mysteriously, production at Plantation Pride stopped in the 1990s. No one knows exactly why. There are rumors that the local health department closed the bakery because of unsanitary conditions. The closing of Plantation Pride Bakery (which also provided the yeast to King Arthur Flour Company) was devastating for bakeries across the country because when they ran out of their bags of salt rising yeast, they had to stop making salt rising bread. And it appeared that they had lost the art of making it the original way.

Here is a version of Kohman's patented recipe for salt rising yeast:

First, obtain a pure culture of the bacterium. Then inoculate a cornmeal-milk starter with this pure culture. At the exact point when the starter has the most foam, gently pour the starter liquid onto a sheet of waxed parchment paper placed on a full sheet pan. Place the sheet pan in a proofer with heat no higher than 120°F overnight or until the liquid evaporates. Scrape the dried flakes into a bowl and pulverize to a powder. Add cornmeal to dilute the dried starter and calcium carbonate powder to keep it dessicated. Bag up this yeast mixture for distribution.

At Rising Creek Bakery failures happen. When they do, we go through frantic steps, such as changing the starter jars, changing our starter recipe from potato to cornmeal/milk or vice versa, and trying a different batch of cornmeal. One of these variables will finally get the starter working again. But often, it is hard to be certain which change had made the difference. Needless to say, salt rising bread is a very persnickety bread.

[Jack] I could tell when the sponge was ready because the whole bakery would smell. Customers would come in and say they could smell that stinking bread while we were making it. That's how I knew it would rise as loaves. To the dough, we'd add sugar, salt, and shortening.

Sometimes, if I saw the sponge wasn't looking as it should, I'd add a teaspoonful of commercial yeast to the 80 quarts of dough. Other than that, we didn't regularly put in any commercial yeast. A good batch of salt rising is like an angel food cake…no big holes in it.

We never add yeast to our salt rising bread; we call that cheating! Salt rising bread made with yeast is so strong that it masks the wonderful, authentic flavor of old-fashioned salt rising bread. Our bread carries on that wonderful "cheesy" taste and smell that salt rising bread enthusiasts cherish.

I got married in 1947. My wife and I bought my dad's bakery in 1955. We ran it for over 30 years. I worked 12 to 13 hours at the bakery on a regular basis, and never had a break for lunch. You just have to stay till the work is done. Then, sometimes after work, I'd walk 18 holes of golf. We never had any children. When I'd get home, why I just went just to sleep. I slept about 7 hours a night, but not in a row. I'd start work at 2:00 a.m., get home after noon, and sleep for 2 to 3 hours. Then I'd get up, and my wife would come home from the bakery to fix supper. After supper, I'd sleep another 3 or 4 hours.

We tried to sell our bakery three times! We sold the bakery for so much money down and so much money a month. Each time, the new owners would run it for a few months, and then give up. It was just too much work for them. After the third sale, we finally decided to clean it up and close shop.

[Jenny] Never have I worked so hard as at my bakery. It's a very physical occupation and I am stronger than I have ever been in my life. Not only do you have to possess much physical stamina, it's also crucial that, as a small business owner, you have an inner confidence that is like a rock wall. Along with this, it's also important to be open-minded and flexible to ride the waves, so to speak, up and down in the first five to ten years of business. Owning this bakery continues to be an incredible character-building experience!

[Jack] People still remember salt rising bread from our bakery, and many people around Lexington are tickled to death to get it. We have a waiting list of people who want it, whenever I get around to making it here at home. We'll call them up after it's baked, and they come right over.

Baker Bill Crum

Another retired baker we interviewed was Bill Crum (his name fits his profession perfectly!) from Olatle, Kansas. He is 10 years younger than Jack Ward, and had owned a bakery outside of Kansas City, Kansas. Bill had originally contacted me (Jenny) through e-mail at Rising Creek Bakery. He was wondering if we had any of the salt rising yeast, which of course we didn't. Bill and I struck up a dialogue about how to make salt rising bread. Here is his story:

Bill Crum (left) and his son in their bakery.

In 1952, I was 12 years old living near Kansas City, Kansas, and I started working in a bakery. I never left the baking world. I began working at Finkemeier's Bakery (German owned), where they had been making salt rising bread since the 1940s. Eventually, I became the owner of Finkemeier's Bakery in 1979. My wife, sisters, brothers, sons, daughters, nieces, and in-laws all had a hand in running that bakery. Salt rising bread was popular back then, and we made it once a week, getting about 40 loaves per batch. We used a salt rising yeast from the King Arthur Flour Company. I used to swear by this product, as it was foolproof. We never had any failures with salt rising bread. Our bakers would set the starter at noon, with a second stage (sponge) set at midnight. The sponge would ferment for 8 to 10 hours, until it was very smelly. The following morning, bakers made the dough, always adding a little commercial bread yeast.

A young Bill Crum, second from left, with his bakery co-workers.

As soon as Bill mentioned that he added commercial yeast to his batches of salt rising bread dough, we knew the fear of failure, for him, was gone! As salt rising bread connoisseurs know, adding commercial yeast greatly diminishes the ole-timey flavor of salt rising bread. But, perhaps Bill and other commercial bakers had some other secrets that enabled their salt rising bread to retain that old-fashioned, authentic taste. Bill ordered salt rising bread from us and commented that the Rising Creek Bakery's salt rising doesn't smell nearly as strong as his did when he baked it.

Bill continues:

> By the 1960s, the demand for salt rising bread died out. The old-timers died,
> young people moved away, and peoples' tastes changed. Huge chain bakeries and
> supermarket bakeries were selling pre-sliced white sandwich breads. All these
> changes hurt our local bakery, and we had to close our shop in 1998. We were
> able to auction off all the equipment. Even today, after all these years, there are
> several aspects of the bakery that I still miss because it was my life. I miss having
> the daily routine, the people we worked with, the customers that came in, and I
> miss working the equipment. By the way, I still work at a local bakery, but only
> part-time.

Van de Kamp's bakeries on the West Coast

For all the millions of people who lived in California from the 1930s to the 1960s, there's
a good chance they remember Van de Kamp's bakery and the salt rising bread that was sold
through its stores. After quite a search, we were able to contact a descendant of the original

owners, Richard R. Frank, in the
spring of 2015. It was his grandfather,
Lawrence Frank, who, with Theodore
Van de Kamp, came up with the idea
of Van de Kamp's bakery, but not until
their destiny had taken some twists
and turns preceding this goldmine of
an idea. First off, the two gentlemen
hadn't known each other very well
until Mr. Frank married Henrietta Van
de Kamp, Theodore's sister.

Bakers hard at work at Van de Kamp's Bakery.

In the early 1920s, these two enterprising men turned to the baking business with a Holland Dutch theme. Originally, the store was on a trailer, which they hauled around. Their logo was a very innovative design symbolizing a windmill, and painted blue and white. Their bakery business was hugely successful, with the iconic Dutch blue windmill that identified the products inside and transported their reputation over decades. Within six years, there were 63 stores, and eventually there were Van de Kamp's bakeries from Los Angeles all the way up to Seattle, Washington. The bakery then morphed into a bakery/restaurant (a very lucrative business model even for today!).

It wasn't until the later years of Van de Kamp's legacy that salt rising bread was sold. Our searches to obtain their salt rising bread recipe have brought mixed results and more than one recipe, including both a cornmeal/milk and a potato/water recipe. Since these recipes are similar to those we have discussed elsewhere, there's no need to repeat. Whichever recipe was "the one" most commonly used, past employees have documented that there was a strong smell at the bakery during the starter stage. Van de Kamp's was sold to a baking conglomerate in 1956 and continued in business until 1990.

Display ad in *The Los Angeles Times*, March 16, 1959

For a new lift in flavor, Van de Kamp's old-fashioned Salt Rising Bread is the easy answer for jaded appetites, making the taste of bread come alive again at every meal. It's the salt-rising yeast, of course, that puts that superbly different, cheese-like aroma and flavor into every loaf...the loaf that is firm, compact, solid—so fine-textured that each slice seems custom-baked to make perfect, golden toast...toast that takes to butter naturally, with lip-smackin' goodness. Salt-Rising Bread makes so many other foods taste even better...in sandwiches for tea-time snacks, with cucumber slices, water cress, avocado, or good old peanut-butter-and-sweet-pickle...Van de Kamp's is one of the very few bakeries in America that brings you unusual recipes, like old-fashioned Salt Rising Bread... Standard 15 oz. loaf 29 cents.

Memories of Van de Kamp's Salt Rising Bread
Sent to Susan's Salt Rising Bread Project

I grew up in Sacramento, CA, and would visit my grandmother in Southern California when I was a kid. That would have been in the '60s. She had two huge avocado trees in her back yard. We would go to Van De Kamp Bakery in her area and would buy the salt rising bread. As kids, my sister and I were fascinated with the windmill logo that turned and was lit up. You could see it for miles. The

bakery smelled wonderful but it was even better when we would toast the salt rising bread back at the house. It made the whole house "stink" and we referred to the toast as "stinky toast." We would mash wonderful, fresh avocados from my grandmother's trees onto the buttered, still-warm toasted bread for breakfast. A little salt on top. We always looked forward to this breakfast when we would visit my grandmother. We would also buy 4 or 5 loaves of the bread to bring back home to Sacramento, and we would put them in the freezer and use them sparingly. We loved the bread.

On Baking as a Skilled Dance

[Jenny] Throughout this book, we have chronicled how our experiences with making salt rising bread have evolved through the years. As with any profession, and especially when the hours of operation are in the wee early morning hours, a person wants to dance through the required tasks of the day. When I say dance, I am describing all the physical movements the body makes in a bakery. The mixers do the heavy kneading, but that is

just one step in many required to produce artisan bread and delicate pastries. Other steps include bending down often to scoop flour, lifting large bowls with mixtures inside, scaling hundreds of pounds of dough, whisking gallons of custard simmering on a hot stove, rolling out the various laminated doughs and pie doughs, removing large batches of baked goods from the oven. The dance comes when a person knows the steps so well that it becomes almost effortless, as bakers slide past one another in the narrow confines between the equipment and the working table. So, when you have the routine down, and all of a sudden the salt rising doesn't work, but someone has a better idea, there is initial resistance to stopping the dance and trying something new. But this is how innovation happens, changes are made, and the dance momentum is established once again.

❧ TOMATO GRAVY ON SALT RISING BREAD ❧

This recipe comes from Nancy Lyman, otherwise known as Sue McDonald, chef at Rising Creek Bakery, who grew up in Core, West Virginia. This gravy is more like a thick tomato soup and makes a great side dish with breakfast.

INGREDIENTS

4-6 home-grown tomatoes
 (or equivalent canned tomatoes, diced)
Tomato juice, if using canned tomatoes
Salt and pepper to taste
¼ cup butter

4 cups milk, then cream to make
 the best consistency
½ cup flour
2 slices salt rising bread toast
Butter for toast, if desired

PREPARATION

1. Blanch the tomatoes and peel off the skin. Return tomatoes to the pot and cook until soft enough to smash with a potato masher. Remove the water. Add salt, pepper, and butter to taste.

2. In a separate pan, heat the milk, being careful not to scorch.

3. While milk is heating, melt the butter in a separate pan. Add the flour to make a roux, and cook a couple minutes (no need to brown it).

4. Slowly add ½ cup of the heated milk, stirring to a smooth paste before adding more. Keep adding milk this way to avoid lumps.

5. Add the cooked tomatoes and stir to even consistency. Can add more tomato juice, if need.

6. Cook a few minutes until thickened. Add cream to desired thickness.

7. Season with salt and pepper to taste.

8. Arrange slices of toast on a plate and pour tomato gravy over toast.

9. Serve while still warm.

❧ BREAKFAST SANDWICH WITH BACON ❧

People go crazy for this signature sandwich, served with either bacon or ham!

INGREDIENTS

2 slices salt rising bread
Butter for toast, if desired
1 egg
1 slice cheddar cheese
2 slices bacon
¼ red pepper

Italian herbs, salt, and pepper to taste
¼ onion
½ T brown sugar
1 T red wine vinegar
Plain or garlic herbed mayonnaise

PREPARATION

1. Toast the bread (butter slices, if desired).
2. Fry egg over-easy or medium, depending how you like it. Once flipped, place a slice of cheddar cheese on top to melt. Turn off heat.
3 Fry bacon to desired crispness.
4. Lightly sauté red pepper in olive oil until soft. Season with Italian herbs, salt and pepper to taste.
5. Slice onion thinly; coat with brown sugar and red wine vinegar. Caramelize the onion until lightly browned and crispy.

ASSEMBLING THE SANDWICH

1. Spread plain or garlic herbed mayonnaise on 1 slice.
2. Place the egg/cheese on top.
3. Lay bacon slices on top of egg.
4. Arrange the sautéed peppers and onions on top of the bacon.
5. Place the other slice of toast on top. Cut in half.

SMOKED SALMON SANDWICH
WITH SALT RISING BREAD

INGREDIENTS

One small red onion

½ cup red wine vinegar

½ cup water

1 T brown sugar

2 slices salt rising bread

Butter, if desired for toast

3 oz. cream cheese

½ tsp. capers

½ clove garlic

2-3 oz. smoked salmon slices

Spring lettuce leaves

PREPARATION

1. Slice the onion thinly. Combine the vinegar, water and brown sugar. Bring to a boil, then pour over the onions. Let this mixture sit until cooled. Keep in refrigerator.

2. Toast the bread (butter slices, if desired).

3. Combine cream cheese, capers and garlic. Blend until smooth. Taste for pungency.

ASSEMBLING THE SANDWICH

1. Spread cream cheese on one or both slices of toast.

2. Add salmon slices on one slice.

3. Add slices of onion on top of the salmon.

4. Arrange a bed of spring lettuce on top of the onions.

5. Place other slice of toast on top and cut in half.

In Praise of New Ideas: Gluten-Free Salt Rising Bread

(Jenny's quest for a delicious, well-textured loaf)

The demand for gluten-free bread is real. Currently, it is not clear why there is an increase of gluten intolerance. Since working at the bakery, I am found to be one of those sufferers and cannot tolerate ingesting normal amounts of wheat products, namely bread. Hence, my quest for a good-tasting gluten-free bread is personal.

I have tried all the commercial gluten-free bread products on the market and honestly have to say I would rather go without. I know I'm not alone in this feeling. And then there are all the other allergies people have these days. Quite the challenge! Fortunately, gluten-free salt rising bread can be made without any allergens and offers a wonderful alternative. It took me more than a year and many false starts before I developed a recipe that created the taste and texture I was looking for.

What is gluten and what does it do?

Gluten is found in many grains, with wheat containing more gluten than most other grains. Gluten is a composite of proteins that play crucial roles in the wonderful chewy texture and delicious flavor of bread. Gluten proteins form long strands of molecules that become lined up upon mixing and kneading. Once lined up, these strands form layers, kind of like a wall. In yeast breads, the yeast is feeding off the dough, then produces carbon dioxide gas. The gluten walls will stretch and balloon outward from this gas build-up and make your bread dough rise. Salt rising bread is unique because there are bacterial microbes instead of yeast that raise the bread, but the action of the gluten walls is similar. These bacteria feed off the dough, then produce hydrogen gas, as well as carbon dioxide gas. Since hydrogen is lighter than carbon dioxide, the crumb texture of salt rising bread tends to consist of smaller holes and a whiter color – similar to a pound cake!

In gluten-free bread, on the other hand, there are only a few proteinaceous strands that form a barrier to hold gases. Hence, the dough will not rise as much and is of a more crumbly structure. Since gluten-free breads don't use wheat flour, that wonderful flavor that we all love in wheat breads is also missing. Thus, it is important to incorporate a new flavor component that is as good as or even better than what our palate is used to.

Let the Experiments Begin!

Initially, we were looking for a yeast-risen bread recipe that included gluten-free grains and had a delicious flavor profile. (At the time, we weren't thinking about developing a gluten-free salt rising bread, which is yeastless.) A well-regarded physician here in Mt. Morris, Dr. Norihito Onishi, treats many patients who suffer from food allergies, and he sends all his patients to the bakery, where they ask for baked goods without dairy, eggs, nuts, soy, sweetener or gluten. To accommodate this very real need, we started researching and testing a number of gluten-free recipes that were also free of those other allergens.

The first recipes we tested used yeast to raise the dough and various ratios of gluten-free grains, seeds and fruit. We struggled with how to create something yummy without the usual ingredients that make bread taste good. In addition, occasionally someone comes into the bakery and asks for a yeastless bread. So we had our challenge set out for us.

After rejecting the many gluten-free bread recipes that just didn't taste that good (and which included yeast), we had an "aha" moment: We would develop a recipe for a gluten-free salt rising bread, which we knew had great flavor potential. We borrowed from the Greek and Sudanese use of chick peas and lentils for their breads, both legumes being gluten-free – and I reconfigured a formula of gluten-free grains into a starter/sponge/dough recipe that worked. We now have a gluten-free salt rising bread that has a marvelous flavor and texture. I can honestly say I prefer it to many wheat breads!

It has been a steep learning curve. Gluten-free grains result in very different baked products than what is made from regular wheat flour. They have their own set of rules for mixing, for what makes them rise, and for the texture and flavors that are found in the finished product. At Rising Creek Bakery, we hope to offer some solutions for the gluten-intolerant individuals who continue to search for delicious breads and pastries.

A Historical Note

During U.S. participation in World War I (1917-1918) most of the nation's wheat was being utilized for the soldiers, so families on the homefront had to come up with alternative flours for bread and cake. Women were experimenting with rye flour, potato meal and a smaller proportion of wheat to produce what was called "war bread" (or Kriegsbrot in war-torn Germany). A popular cake was made with ground clover meal, horse-chestnut flour and rice flour. Newspapers across the U.S. expounded on the successful flavor, appearance and nutritional value of these products. A hundred years ago, out of necessity, people were adapting to gluten-free diets!

GLUTEN-FREE SALT RISING BREAD

YIELD: 2 TO 3 LOAVES

INGREDIENTS

Boiling water – enough to cover
  the sliced potatoes
3 medium-size potatoes,
  peeled and sliced

¾ tsp. baking soda
¼ cup sugar
¼ cup garbanzo flour
¼ cup cornmeal

PREPARATION

1. Slice the potatoes into a large gallon jar. Place the garbanzo flour, cornmeal, and baking soda on top of the potatoes. Pour boiling water over all to cover the potatoes. Give it a swirl.
2. Cover the jar opening with plastic. Poke a hole in the plastic to allow air in. Place in a warm setting.

SPONGE: *2-3 hours at 104-110° F (40-43°C). Let rise until double and just begins to stink.*

INGREDIENTS

1 cup hot water
1 cup brown rice flour
¾ cup arrowroot flour
¾ cup garbanzo flour

²⁄₃ cup buckwheat flour
½ cup cornmeal
¾ cup potato starch

PREPARATION

1. After the starter has foamed up and is smelly, pour all of the liquid into a large bowl, holding back the potatoes. Add 1½ cups of hot water to the potatoes in the starter jar and swirl it around to get all the ferment off the potatoes and into the liquid. Pour this water into your bowl.
2. Add all the remaining ingredients for the sponge. Cover with plastic and place in a warm place to double in volume.

DOUGH: *In pan for 1-2 hours at 104-110°F (40-43°F) until dough rises slightly above the top of the pan.*

INGREDIENTS

Sponge – use all
¾ cup water
½ cup white rice flour
¾ cup Arrowroot flour
1½ T salt

¾ cup buckwheat flour
⅔ cup cornmeal
1 T psysllium
¾ cup vegetable oil

PREPARATION

1. Add to your sponge all the ingredients in the dough. Mix it for an even consistency. Fill a pan slightly more than half full. Dough is quite wet and needs the sides of the pan to rise up. Let this rise in a warm place until just slightly higher than the sides of the pan. Bake for 15 minutes, turn, and another 10-15 minutes until nicely brown on top.
2. Bake at 325°F (160°C) convection, 350°F (175°C) regular oven.

NINE

Passing It On: A Living Legacy

Featuring Velda Moore of Burton, West Virginia
Nancy Booth of Elkins, West Virginia
Mary Ellen Cobb of Ronceverte, West Virginia

We began our story by seeking out the guardians and inheritors of the rich salt rising bread tradition. We looked to the past for answers to the many mysteries of this remarkable bread, and we looked to modern science to help us understand the behavior of the wild microbes that shape the bread's unique personality. We're ending our story by looking to the future. Who will be the ones to keep the tradition alive and pass it on to new generations of bakers?

Throughout our interviews with the wonderful baking elders you have met in this book – and many others who generously shared their stories with us – we have heard how important it was and is to pass on the knowledge. Knowledge can so easily be lost in the rush of life today. It was Pearl Haines who epitomized for us the way we create a chain of meaningful connections from one generation to the next. If you recall from our interview

with Pearl in Chapter 2, she passed on to her daughters and granddaughters the art of salt rising bread. And today, one of her great-granddaughters has taken up the mantle and is making salt rising bread in the same wooden bowl that Pearl's great-grandfather made in 1869 as a wedding gift for his son's new bride. What history resides in that wooden bowl! What stories of lives centered around the simple act of making bread for the people we love. A priceless heritage.

Susan Passes It On

As a child growing up in a big family, feeling like I was someone special was not something I often experienced. I couldn't have guessed that salt rising bread would be what would make me feel special – but it did, indeed!

I was the one who watched Grandmother make her starter and carefully set it on top of her gas-heated hot water tank to "work" overnight. And I was the one Grandmother teased about my initials being the same as salt rising bread. But most of all, I was the only

Susan's niece, Hope, and daughter, Annie, honing their salt rising bread skills

grandchild whom Grandmother taught, step-by-step, to make her wonderful salt rising bread. Admittedly, I had many failures for many years, but when I finally got it right, as a young mother with family of my own, I knew it was to her I owed my success.

So, when my children were ready to learn how to bake salt rising bread, I was on it! And they were into it! This teaching has taken place over a number of years, in several settings, as they have grown up, gone away to college, and come back home. It has been so much fun to do together. I especially remember the weekend that my children, Sam and

Annie, and my niece, Hope, had their first "official" lesson in making salt rising bread. The girls recoiled at the strong smell of the starter and sponge, even though Annie had grown up with it. But because they both love the toast so much, they stuck with it and are happy now that they did. Knowing that I have taught them all a deep appreciation for keeping this tradition alive and for passing it on to coming generations makes me, once again, feel special…and very lucky!

Velda Moore

If you were lucky enough to be at Velda Moore's home early on this Saturday morning, you would have been privileged to participate in the salt rising bread *"Hurray, It Worked!"* dance.

Five smiling women were happily doing that dance when I (Susan) called Velda that morning to ask if her salt rising bread starter had come. She excitedly told me that not only had it come (at 6 a.m.), but that the women were already making sponges and would soon be making dough. That news sent me immediately on my way to a remote rural area at the far end of Monongalia County, West Virginia, to record this special day's activities.

Anyone who has ever attempted to make salt rising bread and been successful, knows the joy and relief that come over you when you awaken to find a foamy, bubbling, very smelly starter. Sweet success! Velda, of course, has experienced this feeling many,

l. to r.: Velda Moore, Linda Tennant (Velda's daughter), Becky Sanders, Kaye Bartrug and Susan Lewis

many times because she is a master salt rising bread baker. This, in fact, is why she and four smiling young women are in her kitchen on this early winter morning. They arrived at Velda's house the evening before. Velda's daughter Linda, who lives two miles from her mother, and three of her daughter's long-time college friends came from far and wide to

participate in this long-awaited salt rising bread weekend. Arrival on Friday was planned so that each "student" would be present to watch Velda make her salt rising bread starters that evening.

All eyes are all on Velda as she adds flour and water to her sponge, creating in just a few turns with her knowing hands six perfect loaves of salt rising bread dough. They are soft and light, filling the old bread pans to just the right height, leaving exactly enough room for the dough to rise.

While the bread rises, Velda dispenses some of her salt rising bread-making wisdom. "Sometimes, for a shortcut, I'll save a hunk of my dough and put it back in my warm water and my sugar and start it all over again, as if I didn't have a step for the risin'." In other words, she skips the first step (the starter) this way. "Lots of times I have better bread that time. I've tried taking this down to a third try with some of my friends, but when we did that third time, it didn't have the taste and the smell that it should have."

Fitting right in with the weekend's objective of passing on salt rising bread memories, Velda talks about some of the women in her family. "My mother got her recipe from her mother. I'd say the recipe has been passed down for generations. I was born in this house. My mother lived here, and my grandmother lived here. Lots of salt rising bread was baked in this house, lots of it on the old wood stove which was right behind where I'm standing now. I've been making salt rising bread for 50-some years."

Finally, the loaves have risen and are ready for baking, and before we know it, six beautiful, golden, slightly domed loaves fill the air with their sweet, unmistakable salt rising aroma. As I leave this country kitchen filled with these young women eager to carry on this beloved family tradition, I know with certainty that the memories they made this weekend at Velda's house will live in their hearts for years to come.

Nancy Booth

Susan and Nancy Booth

What if you don't have a salt rising bread tradition to pass on? If you're Nancy Booth, you start one!

Nancy Booth lives in Elkins, West Virginia, but she grew up in Glady. Glady cannot rightly be called a town, but rather a settlement in a beautiful, remote part of the state. It consists of just a few houses, nestled among pine-covered hillsides, with one road leading off the main highway. The paved road quickly becomes a dirt road and then just a grassy trail that continues to follow behind the few old remaining farmhouses. There are old apple trees lining the trail that are covered with delicious, ole-timey varieties in the late summer. Bears are a common sight around there and signify just how seldom anyone walks or rides down that trail anymore. The last time Jenny was in Glady, she saw evidence of a bear as she was cycling into the entrance to the Monongahela National Forest, which is how Glady is best known today.

On our visit to Nancy in her home in Elkins, she tells us the story of how she first learned about salt rising bread:

> It was in Glady that I first tasted salt rising bread, from my neighbor, Clarecy Whitecotton. This had to be the late 1930s. I was just a little girl, about five years old, and would ask her for some bread, but she would only give me just one slice. She made two loaves at a time using her wood stove. When she made salt rising bread, it smelled all over her house and into ours. Ever since then, I yearned for salt rising bread. You never forget that smell or the taste.

Nancy was young and ambitious and raising her family in the early 1960s when she got the urge to taste salt rising bread again. She knew she had to make it herself if she wanted to eat it. She went back to Glady to see Clarecy Whitecotton, who must have been in her 70s by then, and asked her how the bread is made. Perhaps Clarecy didn't want to share her recipe; Nancy tells it like this: "Clarecy said to take a pinch of this and a handful of that, and I couldn't figure out what she was talking about. It was too complicated!"

Whatever the reason, Nancy wasn't giving up. She and her family were avid readers of the Encyclopedia Britannica. At the time, members could send in an inquiry for specific information, so one day they ordered a recipe for salt rising bread. The recipes arrived in a long, manila envelope and were sourced from cookbooks of the 1930s and 1940s.

Nancy has kept these same recipes in the same envelope in her home for over 60 years. These are the recipes that she still uses today for making salt rising bread. That's one way to start a salt rising bread tradition!

Mary Ellen Cobb

Not everyone who bakes and loves salt rising bread is able to pass it down to children and grandchildren. Family members may love eating it, but may not be natural bakers themselves or their lives are just too busy to spare the time needed for baking it. In Mary Ellen Cobb's case, she is content to share her salt rising bread recipe with her community in Ronceverte, West Virginia. Here is her story:

> *I grew up in Russell County, Virginia, in the town of Belfast. My Aunt Lou made salt rising bread there. She lived on the mountain, up a dirt road, high up on a hill. My mother didn't make it then because my father died when I was six, and my sister was four. My mother was 26, so she had a lot of responsibility. She had cows to milk and all, so she didn't have time to make it. But, I enjoyed eating it when I was growing up.*

Mary Ellen's story begins with a similar scenario of women in the late 1800s, who made salt rising bread. In the diary of Lucy Rebecca Buck of Virginia, recorded on June 13, 1863, she, too, had cows to milk and salt rising bread to bake. Here she writes:

> *Finished ironing, got dinner, and did some cleaning up. In the afternoon, there were pies to make for tomorrow, salt rising to bake, and supper to get besides milking and washing the children. Oh such a weary time as we had of it – the children were sleepy and fretful, the stove wouldn't get hot, the bread would not bake, and the cows would run.*

Luckily for Mary Ellen, she didn't have to contend with recalcitrant cows, but as a young married woman she did have children to take care of. Like many other women at the time, she baked bread, though not salt rising bread at first.

I started making yeast bread before I made salt rising bread. But, when my second daughter had encephalitis and had been in the hospital for three weeks, your [Susan's] Aunt Ann came over and brought me a loaf of salt rising bread. Lou Ellen [Mary Ellen's daughter] said, "Oh, Mom! That bread is so good! Can you make it?" Then I started making it. I won first prize for it at the West Virginia State Fair for many years.

The State Fair had a category just for salt rising bread. I found several of my ribbons. One year, I gave my recipe to my mother-in-law, and she entered it at the fair, and she won the blue ribbon! She was so happy.

Mary Ellen Cobb

At the end of our visit, Mary Ellen laments the fact that she has not taught her family to make salt rising bread, but there is no doubt in our minds that she has, nonetheless, given them a love, appreciation and lifelong memories of this family tradition that they will hold dear. And who knows – maybe one day someone in her family will look for that recipe and restart the legacy.

Homemade bread contests have long been a favorite part of local fairs. In West Virginia, salt rising bread has been a part of the food competition for many, many years. In fact, today, if you attend the West Virginia State Fair in Fairlea, you will find a salt rising bread category in the baked goods section. And if you are the lucky first-place winner, you receive a whole $6.00!

It has always been about a culture of sharing. Throughout the history of making salt rising bread, women have relied on a neighbor, friend, or relative to give them advice about making the bread. In fact, it was not uncommon for a woman to receive from a friend some starter to which she added flour and water, thus ready to set her own salt rising bread starter for making into bread the next morning. Sometimes, women would even give away a wad of their salt rising bread dough, which her friend or relative could then use to begin her starter. The WPA Federal Writers' Project Collection, written in 1936 by Zaidee Walker Miles, describes pioneer women heading into Dixie from Utah: "Salt rising bread was the most common kind in use, and neighbors frequently exchanged emptyins' in order to get a start."

Velda Moore told me that years ago her mother would send some dough to relatives and neighbors by way of the mailman, giving the recipient a start for her salt rising bread. "You wouldn't get your mailman to take it today," Velda laughed. "Often, Mother would put dough in a bread bag or wax paper, and the mailman would take it down the road to my great aunt and put the dough in her mailbox. Mother would call her and tell her it was on its way, and then my aunt would bake bread."

And so, in all these ways and more, the story of salt rising bread is passed on – through that special bond of sharing that devoted bakers understand so well.

ॐ

Closing Thoughts

During the years that we have had the pleasure of meeting and talking with countless people who hold dear their memories of salt rising bread, their words and emotions often left us wishing that we could stay longer… hear just one more story. We contemplate what it is about salt rising bread that can elicit in people such deep longing. And why the memories still linger so many years later. We hope that, because we have persevered with our project, the true knowledge and stories of salt rising bread have not been lost forever, and that others will be inspired to keep the tradition alive.

We continue to pass on the salt rising bread legacy by speaking engagements and salt rising bread classes, and through Rising Creek Bakery in Mt. Morris, Pennsylvania. For news of our appearances, for the latest research, and to read more stories from baking elders and salt rising bread lovers everywhere, please visit Susan's Salt Rising Bread Project online (www.saltrisingbread.net). Do you have a story of your own? We invite you to join the Salt Rising Bread Project's ongoing survey. If you are ever in our corner of the world, please drop by the bakery and say hello.

Milestones and Small Moments on the
Salt Rising Bread Timeline

1778 to Today

1778: Earliest salt rising bread recipe that Susan and Jenny have found, titled "Salt Risen Bread" (A recipe handed down in one family; part of a later published collection of recipes)

1833: Earliest contemporaneously published recipe, "Receipt for Making Excellent Bread Without Yeast" from *The American Frugal Housewife*, Mrs. Lydia Child, facsimile 12th edition enlarged and corrected by the author, 1833; Applewood Books: Boston.

1839: Salt rising "yeast" is first mentioned in a cookbook.

"Salt rising yeast proves convenient when you get out of the other kinds; it does not rise quite so soon as the hop yeast, yet it makes excellent bread"; from *The Kentucky Housewife*, Lettice Bryan, facsimile 1839 edition; Image Graphics: Paducah KY.

1855: Salt rising bread made by Mrs. W. Hamilton: "Awarded at the Third Annual Fair of the Allen County Agricultural Society." *Dawson's Fort Wayne Daily Times*, October 18, 1855.

1863: Lucy Rebecca Buck, of Virginia, writes in her diary: *"Finished ironing, got dinner, and did some cleaning up. In the afternoon, there were pies to make for tomorrow, salt rising to bake, and supper to get besides milking and washing the children."* June 13, 1863.

1873: Salt rising bread said to be superior to common yeast bread and considered by some as more wholesome. "Salt-Rising Bread," *Williamsport Warren Republican*, IN, November 20, 1873.

1876: *April 16:* A reader's request for a salt rising bread recipe sent to The Household section, *The New York Times:* "...I have looked in vain for any inquiry or information about making salt-rising bread..."

August 12: Letter to the editor, *Chicago Daily Tribune,* regarding an article titled "Salt-Rising Bread." September 16: A reader's (Betsy) reply, with recipe.

1877: Salt-rising bread recipe by Mary Gold, *Chicago Daily Tribune,* July 28, 1877.

1879: Salt rising bread recipe in *Housekeeping in Old Virginia,* Marion Cabell Tyree, facsimile reprint, Favorite Recipes Press, Louisville KY.

1886: Recipe for "Salt rising bread," from Abigail Scott Duniway, in *The Woman Suffrage Cook Book.*

1889: Women up in arms over winner of the best salt rising bread at the Manchester Fair in Ohio. "Housewives at War," *The New York Times,* September 15, 1889.

1895: Housewife enquires about which brand of flour makes the best salt rising bread with the least failures, in *The Ohio Farmer.*

1897: Letter to the editor from E.W. Neuman: "He Sighs for Mother's Bread," *The Washington Post,* June 7, 1897:

"Why does not some baker in this town learn how to make 'salt-rising' bread and bake it? Why do they persist in making this sour stuff they sell for baker's bread? That man who has not eaten a toast made of sweet, delicious 'salt-rising' light bread cannot read the 'Book of Ruth with any degree of edification, for I warrant that grain Ruth gleaned in the field of Boaz never came in contact with hop yeast or alum baking powder, of which much of the stuff called bread in Washington is made. Staff of life, indeed! Bah!"

1909: Kansas Governor Walter Stubbs extols the benefits of salt rising bread:
"Nothing will bring more love into the home—the kind that endures—than salt rising bread on the dining room table." Article titled "Boom for Salt-Rising Bread: Kansas Housewives Follow the Lead of Gov. Stubbs," *The Washington Post,* July 11, 1909.

1912-1920s: Dr. H. A. Kohman's research into salt rising bread reveals that a bacterium is responsible for raising the bread and that the gases produced by the bacteria are hydrogen and carbon dioxide. He investigates the various conditions that ensure a successful batch.

1912: Winona Woodward's master's thesis on salt rising bread at the University of Missouri verifies how temperature and bacterial cultures are crucial variables in successfully making this bread.

1915: Dr. Kohman's salt rising bread yeast is patented and large batches start to be sold to commercial bakeries. The potential market to home bakers is not considered at this time to be large enough to address.

1917: Article in *The New York Times* stating that salt rising bread often did not work for home bakers, and the reason may be due to the bacteria that causes the rising.

1918: Kohman's Improver is patented.

1936: WPA Federal Writers' Project Collection, by Zaidee Walker Miles, describes pioneer women heading into Dixie from Utah and making salt rising bread, with neighbors frequently exchanging emptins in order to get a start.

1939: Roland Industries begins selling salt rising yeast, after buying the rights from Kohman.
May 14: "Bread of Salt Rising Type Is Hard to Make," Mary Meade, *Chicago Daily Tribune.*

1959: Van de Kamp's Bakeries in California begins selling salt rising bread.
"Van de Kamp's is one of the very few bakeries in America baking old-fashioned Salt Rising Bread...Standard 15 oz. Loaf 29 cents." (display ad, Van de Kamp's Bakeries, *Los Angeles Times*, March 16, 1959)

1965: Plantation Pride begins selling salt rising yeast after buying the rights from Roland Industries.

1975: King Arthur Flour purchases salt rising yeast from Plantation Pride and starts to market and sell to home bakers.

"If You Don't Want to Make Salt Rising Bread," Craig Claiborne's De Gustibus column, *The New York Times*, December 8, 1975 (article includes recipe).

1984: "A Comforting Companion for Baking at Home," Phyllis Chasanow-Richman, *The Washington Post*, November 25, 1984.

1995: Salt rising yeast no longer commercially available, causing many bakeries and home bakers to stop making salt rising bread.

2010: Rising Creek Bakery opens its doors and ships salt rising bread throughout the United States.

"I Love This Bread..."
more fond memories and appreciations

Susan's Salt Rising Bread Project Gets Mail

Since the Salt Rising Bread Project began, I have been deeply touched by the heartfelt messages that come to my inbox from people who want to share their stories with me. For so many people, salt rising bread acts like a time capsule of treasured memories, connecting them to loved ones from the past or special moments of happiness. I have selected only a few, since I could fill another book with all of them – and I continue to receive these wonderful messages, like the ones below:

> Just a day before our mother took sick and went to the hospital, she had made 8-10 loaves of salt rising bread. She always kept the bread in a huge stone crock with feedsack cloth to keep it fresh. When we kids knew that Mom was not coming home from the hospital, we rationed every piece of bread among us because we knew we would never get any like it again.

I grew up in Kentucky, and when my family would go fishing each weekend on the Salt River, we would take fried chicken, salt rising bread and potato chips. That was all we needed for a fantastic, wonderful meal on the riverbank.

Many a day was spent eating stinky bread with my great aunt and then passing it down to my children and some of their friends. I always laughed when someone new would come in when we were toasting the bread and ask us who was sick. My son, who lives across the state, sent me your website and asked me to make some so we could eat it together like we used to. *At times I feel he doesn't know I am alive, and then he does this and makes me cry.*

I was born in Elkins, WV. My mother made salt risen bread and I took it to school for lunch. I remember that I sure would like to have some store-bought bread like the other kids in my class. Now, I wish I could have just one slice of her salt risen bread. I gave my mother's recipe to friends to bake but it never was as good as my mom's.

I grew up fond of salt-rising bread. It may have been as much about the ritual and the magic as the taste. My grandmother would always wait for a hot, sunny spell to make the bread. She'd rise the bread on the back lawn under a red-and-white checkered dish towel. This seemed like alchemy to a kid. A pinch of soda, the potato and the accompanying odd aroma (as her recipe card says, "if it does not have that odd odor, don't use"). Somehow in the hot sun, the magic always happened. She insisted on slicing it very thinly. When my grandmother died, I immediately told my family that I wanted her recipe box so that I could have her salt rising bread recipe.

I was raised summers on Loon Lake (Cohocton & Wayland) in the Finger Lake Region of NY State. Every summer my grandparents shopped in a bakery in Wayland, NY, and we had lots of salt-rising bread. The taste of toasted salt-rising bread can still well up in my mind 40 years later. The smell of it toasting and the wonderful, unique taste in that warm, loving kitchen is a great childhood memory.

A Survey Reveals a Lot About Salt Rising Bread Lovers

When the bakery first opened *[Jenny speaking]*, we hadn't thought of shipping salt rising bread, but soon after, we were inundated with requests. Once shipping became routine,

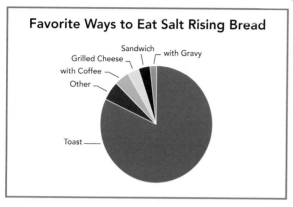

Favorite Ways to Eat Salt Rising Bread

Sandwich
Grilled Cheese — with Gravy
with Coffee —
Other —

Toast —

we included a survey with a bakery-addressed stamped envelope in each box of bread for six months. The survey asked the age of the individual, when and where they first ate it, who baked it, their preferred way of eating it, and a favorite memory about the bread. Of the 100-plus returned surveys, only five of the people were under 60 years of age; their dates of birth ranged from 1920 to 1961. Where were they when they first had salt rising bread? In every corner of the country, in 17 states – with the largest concentration in Appalachia. Who baked it? Lots of grandmothers, mothers, fathers, aunts and friends, as well as the local bakery. The hands-down favorite way of eating salt rising bread? Toast (see the accompanying chart for the runners-up).

Some Favorite Memories from the Survey

- Eating salt rising bread heated on a cast iron skillet, along with bacon, over a campfire, when my great-uncle took me and some other boys camping on the Kentucky River when we were kids.

- The smell at breakfast with the toasting of the salt rising bread.

- After working with my grandfather in the barn, we would come into the house, and he would take a fresh loaf of salt rising bread and tear me off a hunk and hand it to me. We would eat it with fresh tomatoes.

- Bringing it to my grandmother–in-law when she was in the hospital and all the wonderful memories it brought back to her.

- Always having it when I didn't feel good. In later years, we found it at a grocery in Memphis, TN.

- Eating "stinky bread" with family in the 1950s.

- My dad loved it. When I smell it toasting, it brings tears to my eyes and good memories of my dad.

- Eating salt rising bread with my grandfather, born in 1880. We had to take three buses to the bakery to buy it, our little ritual.

Notes of Appreciation

- My wife lovingly ordered several loaves from you for my Valentine's gift. I was moved to tears. Toasting this bread conjures memories of 50-plus years ago when my grandmother made it for me. Please continue creating this most wonderful product!!! Blessings.

- My five loaves of salt rising bread have arrived. It is superb. I can't wait for breakfast each day. Please tell Susan Brown that I would come up there and propose, but I know she must be married.

- I was so excited about receiving my salt rising bread today. It has brought back many, many fond memories of my childhood and well into my adult life. I know it's only bread, but when I was lucky enough to find you on the Internet I could not wait to place my order. It is just like I remember it.

"When nothing else subsists from the past, after the people are gone, after the things are broken and scattered...the smell and taste of things remain poised for a long time, like souls, ready to remind us... bearing resiliently the immense edifice of memory"

– *Marcel Proust,* Remembrance of Things Past

References/Bibliography

American Heritage Editors. 1964. *The American Heritage Cookbook*. American Heritage Publishing Co., Inc. Simon and Schuster, Inc.

Atwater, H.W. 1900. USDA. Farmer's Bulletin No. 112. *Bread and the Principles of*

Barnes, M.J., and Powrie, F. 2011. The Gut's Clostridium Cocktail. *Science*. Vol 331, pp289-290.

Brown, S.R., G. Bardwell. 2015. Salt Rising Bread. Pg. 154-162 in *Handbook of Indigenous Foods Involving Alkaline Fermentation* (Eds. Sarkar, P.K. and Nout, M.J.R.). Boca Raton, FL: CRC Press, Taylor & Francis Group.

Bryan, Mrs. Lettice. 1839. *The Kentucky Housewife. Containing Nearly Thirteen Hundred Receipts.*

Ciullo, P.A. 1954. *Saleratus: The Curious History & Complete Uses of Baking Soda*. Naugatuck, CT: Maradia Press

Clark, D. 1961. The Effect on Salt-Rising Bread of Different Temperature Conditions, Loaf Sizes, and Baking Procedures. Master's Thesis at Cornell University

Danbom, D. 1995. *Born in the Country*. Baltimore, MD: Johns Hopkins University Press

Fisher, Mrs. 1881. *What Mrs. Fisher Knows About Old Southern Cooking.* San Francisco: Women's Cooperative Print.

Furnas, J. C. 1969. *The Americans: a Social History of the United States, 1587-1914*. New York: Putnam

Glasse, H. 1805. *The Art of Cookery Made Plain and Easy*. First American Edition. Alexandria, VA: Cottom & Stewart.

Grinton, William. 2010. *Juliet and Joliet* (1904). Kessinger Publishing, LLC. London.

Hale, S. J. 1841. *Early American Cookery: The Good Housekeeper*. 6th Edition. Boston: Otis, Broaders.

Hartley, M.R. & R.S. Hartley. 2014. *Frontier Table: A Treatise & Source Book on Western Virginia Foodways History 1776-1860*. Parsons, WV: McClain Printing Co.

Hatzikamari, M. et al. 2007. Biochemical Changes during a Submerged Chickpea Fermentation used as a Leavening Agent for Bread Production. *European Food Research Technology* 224: 715-723.

Hatzikamari, M. et al. 2007. Changes in Numbers and Kinds of Bacteria during a Chickpea Submerged Fermentation used as a Leavening Agent for Bread Production. *International Journal of Food Microbiology* 116: 37-43.

Helgason, E. et al. 2000. Bacillus anthracis, Bacillus cereus, and Bacillus thuringiensis – One Species on the Basis of Genetic Evidence. *Applied Environmental Microbiology.* 66(6): 2627-2630.

Holbrook, Delene, 1961. *The Effect on Salt Rising Bread of Different Temperature Conditions, Loaf Sizes, and Baking Procedures,* Cornell University master's thesis. See saltrisingbread.net/index_files/Page437.htm

Horsman, R. 2008. *Feast or Famine: Food and Drink in American Westward Expansion.* Columbia, MI: University of Missouri Press

Jacob, H.E. 1944. *Six Thousand Years of Bread: Its Holy and Unholy History.* Garden City, NY: Doubleday, Doran, and Co.

Juckett, G., G. Bardwell, B. McClane, S.R. Brown. 2008. The Microbiology of Salt Rising Bread. *WV Medical Journal.* Vol. 104. Pp 26-27.

Kohman, H.A. 1912. Salt-Rising Bread and Some Comparisons Bread Made with Yeast. *J. Ind and Eng chem.* 4(1):20-23, 100-106.

Kohman, H.A. 1913. Salt Rising Bread: Raising Dough with Newly Discovered Bacteria. *Scientific American:* Vol. 8, issue 10, pp. 220.

Koser, S.A. 1923. Bacillus welchii in Bread. *J Infect Dis.* 32: 208-219.

McClane, B. 2002. University of Pittsburgh. Unpublished correspondence.

Miles, Z.W. 1936. Pioneer Women of Dixie. Original Paper and given by the author at the Dedication of the Daughters of the Pioneers Monument in St. George, Utah, September 2nd. Library of Congress, Manuscript Division, WPA Federal Writers' Project Collection. http://www.lofthouse.com/USA/Utah/washington/wpa/women.html

Mormon Diary, 1846. Plain but Wholesome: Adventures in Mormon Pioneer Food http://pioneerfoodie.blogspot.com

Nielsen, Reinald S. July 2002. *Petits Propos Culinaires* 70. Salt Rising Bread: A Continuing Conundrum. pp 67-80.

New York Times. 1917. Says Secret Saves Ward Co. Millions. January 20.

New York Times. 1961. Home Breads Rise in Favor. January 20.

Randolph, M. 1860. *The Virginia Housewife Or, Methodical Cook: A Facsimile of an Authentic Early American Cookbook.* Philadelphia: E. H. Butler.

Rubel. W. 2011. *Bread: A Global History.* London, UK: Reaktion Books Ltd.

Sarkar, P.K. and Nout, M.J.R. 2015. *Handbook of Indigenous Foods Involving Alkaline Fermentation.* Boca Raton, FL: CRC Press, Taylor & Francis Group.

Sherfi, A.S. and Hamad, S.H. 2001. Microbiological and Biochemical Studies on Gergoush Fermentation. *International Journal of Food Microbiology* 67: 247-252.

Simmons, A. 1958. *The First American Cookbook, A Facsimile of "American Cookery," 1796.* New York: Oxford University Press, Inc.

The Ohio Farmer. 1895. Salt Rising Bread. *American Periodicals,* May 23, 37, 21, pg 419

The Sun Newspaper, New York. 1909. 2nd section. Boom for Salt Rising Bread

Thorsen, L. et al. 2011. Identification and Safety Evaluation of Bacillus species occurring in High Numbers During Spontaneous Fermentations to Produce Gergoush, a Traditional Sudanese Bread Snack. *International Journal of Food Microbiology* 146: 244-252.

Townsend, Mrs. Grace. 1898. *Imperial Cookbook.*

Warren, F.D. 1895. *The Ohio Farmer.* Housekeeper: Salt Rising Bread. *American Periodicals,* July 11, 63, 1, pg 39.

Woodward, W. 1912. *Bacteria Concerned in the Making of Salt Rising Bread.* Master's thesis, University of Missouri.

Index

Acknowledgments

❧

As we think about all the people who helped us make this book a reality, we first want to thank our families. From Jenny: thank you Sandy, Katy, and Naomi. From Susan: thank you Lee, Sammie, and Annie. Their loving support and confidence in us and in our book were with us all the way.

We also want to thank all the wonderful people at St. Lynn's Press – Paul Kelly, Cathy Dees, Holly Rosborough, Chloe Wertz and Christina Gregory – whose talents and expertise helped us create a beautiful book. We especially wish to thank our editor, Cathy, for her always kind and thoughtful editing.

We thank the photographers, Jason and Elizabeth Bartley of JNB Photo, for their artistic abilities with the camera. Our gratitude extends, also, to Geoffery Fuller for his professional advice and assistance early on. Lastly, to the hundreds of people throughout Appalachia who so kindly let us into their homes and shared with us their salt rising bread recipes, stories, and precious memories: we sincerely thank you. We could not have written this book without you.

About Genevieve Bardwell

Genevieve Bardwell owns and operates Rising Creek Bakery, in Mt. Morris, Pennsylvania, which specializes in salt rising bread and ships hundreds of loaves weekly throughout the U.S.

She graduated from the Culinary Institute of America in Hyde Park, New York, then earned a master's in Plant Pathology.

"It's been a privilege to pass on the legacy of salt rising bread with this book. A privilege, because the elders we interviewed are exceptional individuals of a gentler culture from the past. The portrayals about their youth of sometimes more than a hundred years ago, depicted days aligned with the seasons' rhythms, and time spent working with their hands. Their voices capture memories and a nostalgia for the old-time way of life. We have enjoyed traveling the rural landscapes, driving for miles down the back roads, finally parking our car in a modest driveway. At the front door, we were often met with a noticeable hesitancy or shyness in demeanor. We had invited ourselves into their lives, not the other way around. They needed to check us out, to ensure their words were not going to be laughed at. Once they realized we were serious about salt rising bread, their true, spirited natures came out. And for that we are truly grateful. We are delighted to be able to illuminate an important part of history for you through these people's hearts and kitchens!"

About Susan Ray Brown

Susan Ray Brown grew up in southern West Virginia. She learned to make salt rising bread from her grandmother, whose own mother and grandmother had passed on this time-honored family tradition.

"It is my sincere hope that you, our reader, have enjoyed the stories that we and those we interviewed had to tell and that, in so doing, you have been inspired to find that salt rising bread recipe that you know is somewhere – or to call your sister or your brother, your aunt or your grandmother and laugh, or maybe even cry, as you share your salt rising bread memories. Better yet, I hope that we have inspired you to finally decide to make some salt rising bread yourself! "Passing it on" is an important part of our mission in writing this book. It is as integral to the story of salt rising bread as are the flour and water that create it: one generation teaching the next, telling the stories, and slicing warm salt rising bread fresh out of the oven. It doesn't get any better than that!

"Thank you so much for being a part of this book, whether you told us your story, sent us a recipe, or simply bought the book because you love salt rising bread – or are new to it and are anxious to get to know it better! It's all important and it all plays a part in "keeping the tradition alive."

Other books from St. Lynn's Press

www.stlynnspress.com

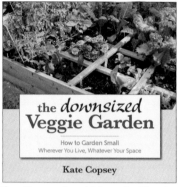

The Downsized Veggie Garden
by Kate Copsey

160 pages • Hardback • ISBN: 978-1-943366-00-2

Ramps
by the Editors of St. Lynn's Press

128 pages • Hardback • ISBN: 978-0-9832726-2-5

Good Mushroom Bad Mushroom
by John Plischke III

104 pages • Hardback • ISBN: 978-0-9819615-8-3

Good Berry Bad Berry
by Helen Yoest

112 pages • Hardback • ISBN: 978-1-9433660-1-9